대학생을 위한

기본영문법

박미숙 지음

BASIC ENGLISH GRAMMAR FOR COLLEGE STUDENTS

신아사

이 책을 쓰면서

이 책은 대학생을 포함하여 영어 문법을 공부하고자 하는 사람이면 누구나 쉽게 이해하고 습득할 수 있도록 구성했다. 각 문법 부분별로 특징적 내용을 정리하였고 선택형과 단답형의 문제풀이를 제시함으로써 영어 문법 지식의 폭넓은 이해를 돕고자 하였다. 특히 문제풀이는 TOEIC과 같은 영어자격 시험과 관련하여 문법의 기초학습능력을 키우고 나아가 영어작문이나 에세이를 쓸 수 있도록 활용 가능한 문법 지식을 함양하는데 도움을 줄 것이다.

이 책에 담긴 문법 내용 설명과 문제들은 중 · 고교 과정의 문법 학습을 넘어 대학생으로서 또는 취업준비생으로서 문법의 기초를 다지게 해 주고 응용된 여러 문법 유형의 문제들을 풀 수 있는 능력을 배양할 수 있도록 이끌어 줄 것이다.

2019년 8월 20일

박미숙

CONTENTS

대학생을 위한

기본영문법

BASIC ENGLISH GRAMMAR FOR COLLEGE STUDENTS

1 명사(Noun)

(1) 명사의 종류

보통명사(common nouns): man, girl, pen, building, book, mice, dog, ⋯

고유명사(proper nouns): John, Korea, Kim, Seoul, Mr. Smith, Cambridge, ⋯

추상명사(abstract nouns): information, knowledge, idea, opinion, courage, ⋯

물질명사(material nouns): soup, paper, bread, banana, milk, sugar, coffee, ⋯

집합명사(collective nouns): family, audience, team, crowd, class, committee, staff, firm, group, herd, enemy, public, company, ⋯

☆ 복수형으로만 사용하는 집합명사: police, the clergy, nobility, peasantry, cattle, people, poultry, ⋯

(2) 단수/복수 취급이 모두 가능한 집합명사

a. Our **staff are** paid monthly. (직원들)

The company's **staff is** on strike. (직원전체)

b. The **government has** decided to increase welfare expenditure. (정부)

The **government are** not satisfied with their working conditions. (공무원들)

c. There **was a** large **audience** at the concert. (청중)

My **audience were** mostly young adults. (청중들)

d. The **committee has** been exploring alternative solutions to the problem at hand. (위원회)

The **committee are** divided in opinion. (위원들)

e. They have a large **family**. (가족)

His **family** have dinner together every weekend. (가족구성원)

(3) 물질명사 용법

① 일반적 물질을 나타낼 때는 관사 없이 사용한다.

Bread is made from **wheat**.

Rice is the chief food of many Oriental nations.

Milk is made into **butter** and **cheese**.

Pepper was very important to Europeans.

② 종류, 개체, 제품 등을 나타낼 때 단수 또는 복수형을 쓸 수 있다.

Is teak **a** hard **wood**? (목재)

A glass is made of glass. (유리잔)

A cigarette was the cause of the fire. (담배 한 개비)

The **waters** of several rivers flow toward Venice. (물줄기들)

③ 물질명사의 수량을 나타낼 때는 단위를 사용한다.

an acre/square mile of land

a bar of soap(gold, iron, chocolate)

a bottle of milk(water, beer)

a cup of coffee(tea)

a glass of water(wine)

a gallon of gasoline(water, milk)

a liter of wine(milk, water)

a piece of advice(clothing, information, machinery, news)

a loaf(slice) of bread

a sheet of paper(metal)

a pound of meat(beef, cheese, sugar, powder)

a spoonful of sugar(salt, pepper)

a tube of toothpaste

two cans of beans / a can of tuna

a bag of sugar / two lumps of sugar

(4) 명사의 소유격 용법

① **생물**: 소유격 [-'s]는 생물체 명사에 붙이는 것이 일반적이다.

Gorge Washington's statue, the boy's new shirt, Daniel's bicycle,
the horse's tail, my sister-in-law's pencil, the lion's hunger

② **무생물**: 대체로 무생물의 소유격은 [of+명사]로 나타내지만 아래와 같이 [-'s]를 사용하는 특정한 경우도 있다.

[of + 명사]: the taste of this medicine(○), this medicine's taste(×)
the noise of the siren(○), the siren's noise(×)
the windows of the house(○), the house's windows(×)

[-'s]: the government's conviction, the nation's social security,
Europe's future, five mile's distance, a brain's total solid weight,
Maryland's Democratic Senator, a week's holiday, today's newspaper

③ **이중소유격**: [of+명사] 형태의 소유격과 [-'s](또는 소유대명사) 형태가 함께 쓰이는 경우를 말한다.

She is **a special friend of mine**.
This poem of Byron's is so beautiful.
Aida is **an opera of Verdi's.**
Biting the nails is **a habit of Sally's**.
A daughter of Mrs. Brown's has arrived.

(5) 명사와 동사의 수의 일치

All the furniture as well as the baggage **is** for sale.
Curry and rice is my usual dinner.
Early to rise and early to bed makes a person healthy.
Two hours is short for us to discuss the matter.
Two-thirds of *the town* was destroyed by the storm.

One-third of *the people* were killed.

All of *the money* was stolen at the market.

All of *the children* in the club **are** nicely dressed.

(6) 셀 수 있는 명사(countable nouns): 보통명사, 집합명사

The trees provide a pleasant shade.

He has to support a large family.

There are four families in this house.

My family are all early risers

Mr. Kim has never spoken to such a large audience.

The audience were all greatly moved by his speech.

The clergy were present at the meeting.

The class is large. / The class are all hard workers.

The police are investigating the murder.

(7) 셀 수 없는 명사(uncountable nouns): 고유명사, 물질명사, 추상명사

accommodation, behavior, furniture, luggage, baggage, news, traffic, advice, bread, information, machinery, permission, work, damage, knowledge, money, scenery, agriculture, cancer, depression, growth, insurance, purity, trade, youth, beauty, finance, marriage, security, welfare, waste, capacity, labor, atmosphere, billiards, economics, diabetes, rabies, physics, politics, …

I'll come back next *Saturday*.

Many *Asians* crossed *the Pacific* to *the United States*.

Wood floats on water but *metal* sinks.

We are anxious for *peace*.

Did you have much *difficulty* finding the house?

Would you like *a loaf of bread* and *a cup of coffee*?

I'd like *a box of cookies*.

We need *three dozen eggs*.

Could you get *two pounds of Swiss cheese*?

Experience is a good teacher.
(cf. She has had many good *experiences* and some bad ones.)

I had *turkey* for lunch.
(cf. Have you ever seen *a wild turkey*?)

Everyone hopes for some *happiness*.

We appreciated your *consideration*.

Mathematics is a difficult subject.

☆ 추상명사나 물질명사의 양을 나타낼 때 little, much, any, some, no 등을 사용.

(8) 특별한 의미를 가진 복수형 명사들

advises	통지	airs	으스대는 태도
authorities	당국, 관계자, 관청	clothes	옷
effects	부동산	expenses	경비
goods	상품	likes	기호
pictures	영화	quarters	지역
riches	부	sights	관광지
manners	태도	arms	무기
refreshments	간식	customs	관세
works	공사	forces	무력, 부대

The *authorities* were called to the scene of the crime.

Authorities say no one survived the second crash, either.

Male prejudice still exists in some *quarters*.

The businessman had a company credit card to pay for his *expenses*.

The rich woman put on *airs* when she was around her friends.
(put on airs: 거만하다, 잘난 체하다)

Police officers in the UK do not usually carry *arms*.

(9) 기타 용법

① the + 단수보통명사: 추상명사로 취급

The pen is mightier than **the sword**. (문(文)은 무(武)보다 강하다)

He felt **the patriot** rise in his heart. (그는 애국심이 마음속에서 일어나는 것을 느꼈다)

② 보통명사 ⓐ + of + a + 보통명사 ⓑ: ⓐ와 같은 ⓑ

He met an angel of a girl.
= He met a girl like an angel.

The millionaire lives in a palace of a house.
= The millionaire lives in a house like a palace

③ 종류 전체를 나타낼 때

The dog(A dog) is man's best friend.
= Dogs are man's best friend.
(The dog, A dog, Dogs는 모두 일반적인 'dog'를 대표한다)

(10) 명사의미 구분

accountant	회계사	account	계산	accounting	회계
applicant	지원자	application	지원	appliance	기구, 장치
attendant	참석자	attendance	출석	attendee	출석자
consultant	상담자	consultation	상담	consultancy	컨설팅사
occupant	점유자	occupancy	점유	occupation	직업
producer	생산자	production	생산	product	생산품
receptionist	접수원	reception	수령	receptacle	그릇, 용기

analyst	분석가	analysis	분석
architact	건축가	architacture	건축술
assembler	조립공	assembly	조립
authority	권위자	authorization	권한부여

beneficiary	수익자	benefit	이익
committee	위원(회)	commitment	위탁, 헌신
consumer	고객	consumption	소비
contributor	공헌자	contribution	공헌
distributor	분배자	distribution	분배
donor	기증자	donation	기증
editor	편집자	edition	발행, 편집
employee	피고용인	employment	고용
engineer	기술자	engineering	공학
founder	설립자	foundation	설립, 재단
manugacturer	제조업자	manufacture	제조업
manager	경영자	management	경영
illustrator	삽화가	illustration	삽화
inspector	검사자	inspcction	검사, 조사
instructor	교육자	instruction	교육
interpreter	통역사	interpretation	통역, 해석
journalist	기자	journal	일지
negotiator	협상가	negotiation	협상
opener	개시자	opening	개시
operator	기사, 운용자	operation	작동
owner	소유자	ownership	소유권
participant	참가자	participation	참여
president	대통령	presidency	대통령직
relative	친척	relation	관계
representative	대표자	representation	대표
resident	거주자	residence	거주
rival	경쟁자	rivalry	경쟁
subscriber	구독자	subscription	구독
supervisor	감독자	supervision	감독

technician	기술자	technology	기술
coverage	(취재, 보상, 적용)범위	cover/covering	표지/덮개
delivery	배달	deliverance	해방, 구조
entry	참가등록	entrance	입장, 입구
identification	신분증명	identity	정체성
interests	이익	interest	관심
likelihood	가능성	likeness	유사성
objective	목표	objectivity	객관성
object	목표, 물체	objection	반대
percent	퍼센트	percentage	비율
permit	허가증	permission	허가
procedure	절차	productivity	생산성
remainder	나머지	remains	유물
responsibility	책임	responsiveness	반응
segment	부분	segmentation	분할
sense	감각	sensation	감동, 흥분
utilization	이용, 활용	utility	효용, 실리

(11) 복합명사

account number	계좌번호	exercise equipment	운동기구
application fee	신청비	expansion project	확장계획
application form	신청서	expiration date	만기일
arrival date	도착일	feasibility study	예비조사
assembly line	조립라인	growth rate	성장률
attendance record	출석기록	interest rate	금리, 이율
client satisfaction	고객만족	investment advice	투자조언
conference room	회의장	keynote speaker	기조연설자
confidentiality policy	보안정책	living expenses	생활비

confirmation number	주문번호	performance appraisals/evaluations	업무수행평가
enrollment form	등록양식	occupancy rate	점유율
exchange rate	환율	quality requirement	품질요구
reception desk	접수처	return policy	반환정책
reference letter	추천서	safety inspection	안전검사
registration form	등록서	sales representative	외판원
repair facility	수리시설	retirement celebration	퇴직기념축하연
research program	조사프로그램	security card	보안카드
retail sales	소매판매	service desk	안내데스크

EXERCISE

Ⅰ. Choose the correct form that would be acceptable in each sentence.

1. A mountain (of / with) a wave struck Japan.
2. He felt (the patriot / patriot) rise in his heart.
3. (A cattle / Cattle) were sold for next to nothing.
4. Penicillin is (a great discovery / great discovery).
5. He has not had (much experience / an experience) in the field.
6. He (got / had) the good sense not to be involved in the scandal.
7. It is the (customs / custom) for Koreans to take off their shoes when they get into a room.
8. The government set up a (five-year / five years) economic development plan.
9. The storm did (a little damages / great damage) to the crops.
10. There has been (a great number of propaganda / a great deal of propaganda) about the dangers of smoking.
11. If anybody (call / calls) me, you can tell them I'll be back soon.
12. Our office is too small so we are looking for a bigger (it / one).
13. The difference between the selling price and cost (is / are) the companies' profit.
14. Although his (occupation / occupancy) was teaching, he dabbled in stock trading.
15. Every (application / applicant) was given an official receipt for fees paid.
16. The manufacturer accepts no (responsibility / responsiveness) for

replacement if the product is broken due to misuse.

17. The (founder / foundation) of the local center reflects the city's commitment to artists and culture.
18. Paul was given the (responsiveness/responsibility) of preparing the equipment needed for the presentation.

Ⅱ. Find an error in the underlined parts of each sentence and correct it.

1. The news of the President's treaty with the foreign government were received with complicated emotions by the citizens of both governments.
2. Daniel said that if he had to do another homework tonight, he would not be able to attend the concert.
3. Mumps are a very common disease which usually affects children.
4. Our new television came with a six-months warranty on all electrical components.
5. If you should want any other information about it, talk to anyone who is the club's member.
6. The ease with which abalone can be collected from the shore has almost resulted in its extinct.
7. Some people make more money than us teachers, but few gain as much satisfaction from their work.
8. We employ scientists who create models of the inventions to see if it works well.

9. We advise people to invest in something that make more money for them.

10. The chairman will announce the opening of the meeting as soon as everybody arrive.

11. Evaluations will be based not only on personal performance, but also employee attending records.

12. All products must be removed from the shelves in accordance with the marked expiring date on each package.

13. A number of my friend are planning to go to Hawaii on holiday this summer.

14. They are supposed to receive one-and-a half time their hourly wage for overtime.

15. Transport is the life-blood of a nation's economy; without it none interchange of goods and people would be possible.

16. The luggage weighs two hundreds and fifty pounds, so the shipping cost will be less than one hundred dollars.

17. Most films are so poor that they are not worth a price of a ticket.

Ⅲ. Choose the best completion for the following.

1. We expect everyone to carry out ____________ duty.

   a. our　　b. there　　c. his　　d. their

2. I didn't choose any of the three offerings, because I found ____________ satisfactory.

   a. neither of them　　b. none of it

   c. either of them　　d. none of them

3. The company cuts the length of its wireless contracts from two years to one year in ____________ to entice more consumers.

   a. effort　　b. an effort　　c. efforts　　d. the effort

4. We've got ____________, but the price is surprising!

   a. a lovely furniture　　b. some lovely furniture

   c. so many lovely furnitures　　d. two piece of lovely furniture

5. It was not until she had arrived home ____________ remembered her appointment with the doctor.

   a. that she　　b. when she　　c. and she　　d. she

6. We are working with a group of ____________ developing a safe way to produce energy.

   a. inventor who is　　b. inventors who is

   c. inventor who are　　d. inventors who are

7. They are disappointed with the sales result at the department store, where operating ____________ was lower than expected.

   a. performance　　b. to perform　　c. performed　　d. perform

8. The Human Resources department organized a half-day workshop for ______________ who want to improve their leadership skills.

   a. them b. themselves c. those d. these

9. Management took financial factors into account when making its ______________ to delay integrating the new software system into the company.

   a. decided b. deciding c. decision d. decisive

10. We would like to thank Mr. Holmes for his ______________ and wish him success in his future endeavors.

   a. contribute b. to contribute
   c. contributing d. contribution

11. If we do not handle ______________ with proper care, our workers and customers may be in danger.

   a. chemist b. chemicals c. chemistry d. chemically

12. One day we will be old enough to retire and will not have to come back to ______________.

   a. work b. a work c. works d. the works

13. Many of the policy holders of National Insurance receive ten percent ______________ for cars or houses covered in their contracts.

   a. discount b. discounts
   c. discounting d. discounted

14. It is common practice today for psychologists to serve as ______________ to toy companies in the design of toys for children of different ages.

   a. consult b. consultations
   c. consultants d. consultancy

15. With nearly two ____________ orders placed within the first day, the manager has decided to add another work shift to meet product demand.

a. thousand　　b. thousands
c. a thousand　　d. thousands of

16. The ____________ equipment at the new fitness club is guaranteed to help men and women achieve greater muscle tone in just a few weeks.

a. exercisable　　b. exercised　　c. exercising　　d. exercise

17. Visitors are not allowed to use the back of the building to park their cars without obtaining a parking ____________ from the attendant.

a. permission　　b. permit　　c. permitting　　d. to permit

18. Some people don't agree that ____________ always the best policy.

a. honesties are　　b. the honesties are
c. an honest is　　d. honesty is

19. Mr. Johnson didn't get the job because he didn't have the right ____________.

a. qualify　　b. qualifying
c. qualified　　d. qualifications

2 동사(Verb)

〈동사유형〉

기본형	현재	과거	미래
	동사원형(-(e)s)	동사의 과거형	will 동사원형
진행형	현재진행	과거진행	미래진행
	am, is, are + -ing	was, were + -ing	will be + -ing
완료형	현재완료	과거완료	미래완료
	have, has + p.p.	had p.p.	will have p.p.
완료진행형	현재완료진행	과거완료진행	미래완료진행
	have(has) been -ing	had been -ing	will have been -ing

I **study** English three hours a day.

Learning English **is** not easy.

The sun **rises** in the east.

This beach **belongs to** the city.

Joe **came** to Canada three months ago.

I'**ll buy** you a new jacket sooner or later.

She **is studying** French this semester.

He **was sleeping** when the phone rang.

What **will** he **be doing** between 3:00 and 5:00?

I **have** already **taken** two Spanish courses.

How many times **have** you **gone** there?

Joe **had finished** the article by 8:00.

I tried to call her, but she **had** already **left**.

They **have lived** in this town for 20 years.

By next year, my daughter **will have started** elementary school.

He **has been studying** here since March.

He **has been living** in Ottawa for three years.

She **had been sleeping** for two hours by 7:00.

She noticed that a man **had been following** her for several blocks.

She **will have been going** to school for 18 years by graduation day.

We **will have been discussing** this problem for two hours by the time he arrives.

(1) 자동사와 타동사로 모두 쓰이는 동사

stand, sell, break, move, pay, write, count, work, walk, run, sing, change, …

He **stood** still. / I can't **stand** the noise.

This book **is selling** well. / Her novel **has sold** one thousand copies in a month.

The Earth **moves** around the sun. / Steve **moved** the desk to his office.

The pen **writes** smoothly. / He **wrote** a book on history.

The fact **counts**. / He **counted** the eggs.

Honesty always **pays**. / He has to **pay** the money to Susan.

(2) 자동사(전치사 동반 가능)로 쓰이는 동사

arrive (at), hope (for), listen (to), reply (to), apologize (to), agree (to, with), complain (of), look (up at, at, for, …), stay (at), wait (for), subscribe (to), object (to), rise, lie, …

He **subscribes** regularly to the charities

I have **subscribed to** the magazine since last year.

I **hoped for** good weather.

We **apologize to** you for our late response.

(3) 타동사(전치사 없음)로 쓰이는 동사

resemble, reach, approach, attend, answer, marry, discuss, consider, offer, explain, contact, enter, address, obey, call, become, mention, survive, leave, raise, lay, …

I don't **resemble** my parents in appearance at all.

How many people **attend** church every Sunday?

I've been trying to **contact** you all day.

(4) 직접목적어+간접목적어

① 간접목적어 앞에 전치사 to를 가지는 동사

bring, lend, pass, sell, take, write, give, offer, read, send, teach, leave, owe, recommend, show, tell, …

Mr. Baker **offered** the job **to** her.

The news **brought** tears **to** his eyes.

I **recommend** the book **to** all my students

② 간접목적어 앞에 전치사 for를 가지는 동사

book, choose, find, keep, prepare, bring, cook, fix, make, save, buy, do, get, order, …

I **bought** some books **for** my friends.

They **brought** presents **for** the baby.

The police **are preparing** themselves **for** trouble at the demonstration.

Why don't you **make** something very special **for** her?

(5) to부정사를 직접목적어로 취하는 동사

advise, persuade, remind, teach, tell, expect, offer, order, propose, recommend, require, request, suggest, want, …

They **advised** me *to take* the job.

He **expected** you *to telephone* him.

I **persuaded** her *to see* a doctor.

True marriage **requires** us *to show* trust and loyalty.

(6) 사역동사

① '~하게 시키다(만들다)'의 뜻을 가진 사역동사 let, make, have, get:
(목적어는 사람, 목적격보어는 동사 원형을 취함)

❶ let, make, have는 목적격 보어로 동사의 원형을 쓴다.

I'll **let** you **know** later.

We can **make** them **understand** the truth.

They **have** the students **wear** school uniforms.

(cf. have는 현재분사형을 목적격보어로 취하기도 한다.
Susan **had** him **waiting** all day long.)

❷ get은 목적격 보어로 to-부정사를 쓴다.

You can **get** someone else **to do** it.

② '~을 당하게(받게) 하다'의 뜻을 가진 사역동사 have, get, make:
(목적어는 사물, 목적격보어는 과거분사형을 취함)

I usually **have** my car **serviced** once a year.

Kate **got** the jeans **burnt** while she was ironing.

(7) 지각동사

지각동사 see, feel, listen to, hear, notice, watch 등은 동사 원형 또는 현재분사형을 목적격보어로 취한다.

They didn't **hear** Ann come in.

I **saw** someone carrying a ladder.

(8) 완료형 조동사 유형

① if절이 없이 과거 사실에 대한 반대를 뜻하는 가정법으로 쓰이는 경우

would have pp: ~했었을 것이다

could have pp: ~할 수 있었을 것이다

might have pp: ~이었을 것이다

should have pp: ~했어야 했다.

We **would have moved** then, but we couldn't find the place that we wanted.

We **could have protested** the building of the factory.

He **might have listened** to our complaints

We **should have sold** our house before the company built the factory across the road.

② 과거 사실에 대한 강한 가능성을 뜻하는 경우

must have pp: 분명히 ~했었을 것이다.

The company **must not have been concerned** about our health and well-being.

(9) 동사의 수동태가 전치사와 함께 쓰이는 경우

be accustomed to	be equipped with
be based on	be filled with(by)
be composed of	be formed of(from, by)
be connected to	be involved in(with)
be covered with	be known for(as)
be derived from	be known to + 동사
be designed for	be linked to
be developed for(with)	be located in(at, on)
be made of(from)	be made up of

be noted for
be shown in(at, on)
be used for(as, with)
be related to
be suited for
be used to + 동사
cf) be used to + 명사(~에 익숙해 있다)

(10) 제안, 요구, 명령, 주장

제안, 요구, 명령, 주장을 뜻하는 동사가 이끄는 종속절은 **(should)+동사**를 취한다.

advise, ask, command, require, urge, demand, insist, desire, propose, recommend, request, suggest, …

We **asked** that the manager attend the meeting.

We were going to **request** that the vice president participate.

We **demand** that something be done about these problem.

We **desire** that everyone be aware of the problem.

EXERCISE

I. Choose the correct form that would be acceptable in each sentence.

1. I'm sorry I'm late. I have (been to / gone to) the dentists's.
2. John (lives / has lived) in Japan now. He (was / has been) there for the last six months.
3. He (was / has been) in the army for 2 years. (He's still in the army)
4. I didn't laugh at the joke because I (had heard / have heard) it.
5. China's economic growth rate (has been declining / have been declining) after the global economic depression.
6. Allan (caught / had caught) a cold because he (had / had had) too much ice cream.
7. What I (was trying / have been trying) to explain at the last seminar was not clear.
8. She (has lived / lived) in this town for thirty years.
9. Three boys (have been waiting / waited) for her in the heavy rain since last night.
10. I (told / said) that the man was a fool but you wouldn't listen to me.
11. He (sat / set) the boxes of fruit down and looked around for someone to help him carry them.
12. Can you tell me what this word (means / is meaning)?
13. Please give him the message if you (see / will see) her.
14. I am accustomed to (spend / spending) a lot of time outdoors.
15. He was (such a poor speaker / such poor a speaker) that we fell asleep.

16. It is essential that you (might / should) take your passport.

17. The road was very dangerous; somebody (should warn / should have warned) us.

18. I've already told the others, so you needn't (to tell / tell) them.

19. Mike and I used to meet regularly but I (haven't had / didn't have) much contact with him recently.

II. Find an error in the underlined parts of each sentence and correct it.

1. After rising the flag to commemorate the holiday, the mayor gave a long speech.

2. Since no ammonia fumes are detected, this theory does not seem credibly.

3. Imagine my surprise when I saw one man in the car pulled out a pocket book and begin to read.

4. Bill's professor had him to rewrite his thesis many times before allowing him to present it to the committee.

5. Despite the roadblock, the police allowed us enter the restricted area to search for our friends.

6. If you stay over four years in the United States, you will have to get your visa extend to four more years.

7. It is difficult to do generalizations about the characteristics of modern music because of the variety of existing styles.

8. The Smiths asked me to look over their plants while they were away on vacation.

9. The athlete was disqualified from the tournament for participating at an illegal demonstration.

10. It is very cozy in here, but the draperies are not hanged well.

11. Financial institutions are able to create, exchange, provision, and utilize funds.

12. The food that Mark is cooking in the kitchen is smelling delicious.

13. The meeting discussed about your request for extension of credit.

14. The company would prefer negotiating directly rather than use an intermediary.

15. Portuguese is seeming harder to understand than Spanish.

16. Employees are likely to achieve greater job satisfaction and performing better if they identify their interests with those of the company.

17. We recommended that he disconnects electricity before he started mending the light switch.

18. The bus was full of people who have spent a happy hour in the stores doing their Christmas shopping.

Ⅲ. Choose the best completion for the following.

1. We will not be ____________ by John's decision, but he will not become aware of that fact for several weeks.

   a. affected b. effected c. brought d. impressed

2. Despite the alarming report of earth tremors nearby, the workers ____________ to lay the foundation of the building.

   a. preceded b. placed c. came d. proceeded

3. A: Bob must be very wealthy.

   B: Yes. He ____________ more in one day than I do in a week.

   a. has been earned b. had earned

   c. earns d. has earnings

4. The cyclist ____________ he crossed the main street.

   a. looked very caution after b. had looked cautiously before

   c. was looked cautious when d. looks cautious when

5. A: There is a movie at the Student Hall tonight?

   B: ____________.

   a. Do you go? b. Did you go?

   c. Are you going? d. Have you gone?

6. Our boss went fishing after he ____________ the conferences.

   a. had finished b. has finished

   c. finishes d. would finish

7. As soon as Pete had arrived, he told us that he ____________ for London after the board meeting.

   a. will be leaving b. would be leaving

   c. left d. had left

8. Everybody was made ____________ it again.

a. examine
b. examined
c. to examine
d. examining

9. The volume of trade between the two countries ____________ very fast.

a. rise
b. is rising
c. is risen
d. have risen

10. We posted the letter to them two weeks ago, but we ____________ a reply yet.

a. aren't going to receive
b. wouldn't receive
c. haven't received
d. hadn't received

11. Before she joined in our company, she ____________ for a long time as an investment counselor.

a. has worked
b. had been working
c. had been worked
d. has been working

12. Providing the quality of the goods ____________ up to our expectations, we can probably let you have regular orders.

a. comes
b. will come
c. came
d. will be coming

13. Mary has little experience in this field, so it ____________ be easy for her.

a. used to
b. cannot
c. must not
d. need not

14. I haven't decided yet but I might ____________ the reception tomorrow.

a. have attended
b. attend
c. have been attended
d. be attended

15. You ____________ me to say you were going to be late.

a. might as well telephone
b. should have telephoned
c. have to telephone
d. have telephoned

16. Advertisers pay to have their messages ____________ by television and radio stations.

a. broadcast
b. broadcasting
c. to broadcast
d. being broadcast

17. Many of the world's essential raw materials ____________ only in one or two special regions.

a. found
b. founded
c. are found
d. are founded

18. I used ____________ running every morning when I was in London.

a. to
b. to go
c. go
d. to going

3 형용사(Adjective)

(1) 형용사(Adjective)

모양, 성질, 크기, 색깔, 수량 등을 나타내는 말로서 대체로 명사 앞이나 뒤에서 수식하지만 명사 수식 없이 동사 뒤에 놓여 서술어로 쓰일 때도 있다.

kind, new, white, interesting, wooden, Japanese, old, angry, excited, noisy, many, much, little, few, five, fifth, …

① **한정용법:**

What is his new *message*? I need *something* new

한정적 용법으로 사용되는 형용사:

atomic, digital, chief, complete, main, only, joint, live, indoor, eastern, western, northern, southern, …

ⓐ 명사 앞에서 한정: only, main, upper, outer, inner, former, latter, elder, short, lazy, fierce, …

ⓑ 명사 뒤에서 한정: anything interesting, a man beloved, everybody everybody imaginable

Would you like to drink something cold?

There was nothing useful in her locker.

② **서술용법:**

John is intelligent.

Sam is good at playing soccer.

His speech made me excited.

Nick is not alone.

These crocodiles are alive.

The performance was worth.

서술적 용법으로 사용되는 형용사:
(서술적 용법의 형용사는 명사 앞에서 그 명사를 수식할 수 없다.)

alone, alive, awake, asleep, alike, afraid, ashamed, aware, unable, worth, pleased, sorry, ready, well, content, glad, …

(2) 한정용법과 서술용법에서 각각 다른 뜻으로 쓰이는 형용사:

	한정용법	서술용법
concerned	걱정하는	관련된
involved	복잡한	관련된
present	현재의	출석한
proper	적절한	본래의
certain	어떤	확신하는
late	세상을 떠난, 최근의	늦은
right	오른쪽의	옳은

A *certain* friend of his teaches politics at university.
I am *certain* that they are ready to help us.

A few brief comments are sufficient for *present* purposes
Mary is *present* at the meeting.

We are receiving a lot of calls from *concerned* friends.
Do you know the names of the people *concerned*?

(3) 형용사를 포함한 한정사의 순서

관사 > 수사 > 크기(형태) > 성상[1] > 신구 > 색깔 > 연령 > 재료 > 목적

These two thin red paper clips are from Japan.

1 성상형용사: 피수식어의 크기, 성질, 상태, 기원(leather, plastic, surprising) 등을 나타내는 대부분의 형용사를 말하며, exciting, excited 등과 같은 현재분사나 과거분사형도 포함된다.

The long winding path to the house was very dark.

His father's large beautiful 1990 Porsche, which is outside, has a dent in it.

That tall nice new student is coming for dinner.

My bag is *a large black leather one*.

I saw her in *an old French film*.

Sue is *the tall young girl*.

I'll be visiting New York for *the first two weeks* of March.

(4) 형용사가 주격보어로 사용될 때 to 부정사를 수반

brave, careless, clever, easy, friendly, generous, good, polite, thoughtful, kind, rude, intelligent, difficult, hard, pleasant, possible, …

You are kind to tell me where I should take a taxi.

She was thoughtful to remind him that we moved into a new office.

cf) It is **kind of you** to tell me where I can take a taxi.
It was **good of him** to see me off at the station.

Their attitudes were difficult to understand.

The place is easy to find.

cf) It was **difficult for us** to understand their attitudes.
It is **important for you** to exercise regularly.

(5) 감정을 나타내는 동사가 과거분사로 쓰일 때 형용사로 취급될 수 있으며 이 때 전치사를 동반할 수 있다.

amazed (at)	excited (about)	satisfied (with, about)
astonished (about)	exhausted (from)	bewildered (about)
fascinated (with)	scared (of)	bored (with)

frightened (about)	shocked (about)	concerned (with, about)
frustrated (with)	stimulated (by)	confused (about)
interested (in)	stunned (about)	convinced (about)
intrigued (with)	surprised (by, at)	determined (to)
perplexed (with)	tired (of)	disappointed (about)
pleased (with)	upset (about)	worried (about)
disgusted (about)	reassured (by)	encouraged (about)

* The movie scared me. / I was scared by the movie. / I was scared of the mask man.

(6) 이성적 판단이나 감정을 나타내는 형용사가 이끄는 강조구문의 종속절에서 should + 동사, 혹은 동사원형이 쓰인다

advisable, imperative, best, important, crucial, necessary, desirable, urgent, essential, vital, admirable, astonishing, regrettable, strange, alarming, embarrassing, remarkable, surprising, amazing, odd, sad, …

It was **vital** that she should make a decision immediately.

It is **advisable** that you should make a scientific approach to this subject.

It was **urgent** that they discuss the matter.

It is **essential** that people be made aware of employment issues.

It is **important** that employers not discriminate against women or minorities.

It is **necessary** that the company should try to hire people from all parts of the population.

감정을 나타내는 일부의 형용사들(admirable, astonishing, regrettable, strange, alarming, embarrassing, remarkable, surprising, amazing, odd, sad)은 시제일치에 따라 술어를 쓰기도 한다.

It is regrettable that you are still waiting for a reply.

It was strange that no one had noticed the warning.

(7) 비슷한 유형으로 주의해야 할 형용사

imaginable 상상할 수 있는	imaginative 상상력이 풍부한	imaginary 가상의
literal 문자 그대로의	literary 문학의	literate 학식 있는
sensitive 민감한	sensible 분별력 있는	sensor 감각의
respectful 공손한, 존중하는	respectable 존경할만한	respective 각각의
industrial 산업의	industrious 근면한	
comparable 비교할 수 있는	comparative 비교의	
considerate 사려 깊은	considerable 상당한	
credible 믿을만한	credulous 속기 쉬운	
contemptuous 멸시하는	contemptible 멸시할만한, 경멸적인	
economic 경제의	economical 경제적인	
desirous 바라는	desirable 바람직한	
successful 성공적인	successive 연속적인, 계승하는	
comprehensive 포괄적인	comprehensible 이해할 수 있는	
reliable 신뢰할 수 있는	reliant 의존하는	
intellectual 지적인	intelligent 총명한	
continual 빈번한	continuous 계속적인	
historic 역사적으로 중요한	historical 역사상의	
satisfactory 충족시키는	satisfying 만족감을 주는	
favorable 호의적인	favorite 가장 좋아하는	
prospective 장래의	prosperous 번영하는	
profitable 유리한, 이익이 많은	proficient 능숙한	
persuasive 설득력 있는	persuaded 확신하고 있는	
beneficial 유익한	beneficent 인정 많은	
appreciable 상당한	appreciative 감사의	
argumentative 논쟁적인	arguable 논박할 수 있는	
informed 정통한, 알고 있는	informative 유익한	

a. Investors watched the rate of **economic** growth.
This is **economical** way of heating my room.

b. It is **sensible** of you to take his advice.
She is very **sensitive** to the cold.

c. These technological developments were hardly **imaginable** 30 years ago.
In modern education, an **imaginative** approach is preferred.

d. She is always polite and **considerate** towards her employees.
The project wasted a **considerable** amount of time and money.

e. Drinking green tea is said to be **beneficial** to the body.

Beneficent people often donate money to poor people.

f. We are looking for someone who is **reliable** and hard-working.

They are not wholly **reliant** on Western charity.

(8) 수량을 나타내는 형용사

셀 수 있는 명사(복수) 한정	셀 수 없는 명사(단수) 한정
many, a few, few, only a few several a number of a great number of a large(huge, considerable) number of a good number of hundreds(thousands, millions) of a variety of	much, a little, little, only a little a great amount of a large(huge, considerable) amount of a great deal of
a lot of, lots of, plenty of, some, any * every, each는 셀 수 있는 명사 앞에서 쓰이며 단수취급	

His sentence contained **a number of grammar mistakes**.

The government has spent **a great deal of money** trying to solve this problem.

Millions of people fly on airplanes every year.

A huge number of people visit Niagara Falls each day.

It takes **a considerable amount of time and effort** to learn a new language.

At the market, you can buy **a wide variety of products**.

(9) 수사를 이용한 관용적 표현

ten to one, nine times out of ten 십중팔구

second to none 첫째가는

second only to ~다음으로 첫째

every other day, every second day, every two days 하루 걸러, 이틀마다

last but one 마지막에서 두 번째

<기타 수사 표현>

4 $\frac{2}{3}$(분수) four and two thirds

¾ three fourths, three quarters

-17℃ seventeen degrees below zero Centigrade

60˚F sixty degrees Fahrenheit

(10) 가산명사, 불가산명사와 함께 쓰는 한정형용사

① 가산명사의 단수형과 함께 쓰는 한정형용사:

another, any, each, either, every, neither, no

I have **another appointment** tomorrow.

The bus comes ten minutes after **every hour**.

② 가산명사의 복수형과 함께 쓰는 한정형용사:

all, any, both, few, many, most, no, other, several, some

Several companies are working together with the project.

Most people realize only a small part of their potential.

③ 불가산명사와 함께 쓰는 한정형용사:

all, any, little, most, much, no, some

You can ask me if you need **any help**.

There lay **much difficulty** in the way.

(11) some, any, another, every, each, both, either, neither, …

Every man had a weapon. (implies that the speaker counted the men and the weapons and found that he had the same number of each)

Each man had a weapon. (implies that the speaker went to the each man in turn and checked that he had a weapon)

Everything has been wasted. (=All the things have been wasted.)

Both (doors) were open.

Both of us knew him. (=We both knew him.)

We ate **all the cakes/all of them/them all.**

We are **all** waiting. You must **both** help me.

Each of us has a map. (=We each have a map.)

I've read **neither** of these books. (=I haven't read either of these books.)

I tried both keys but **neither** (of them) worked.

Neither of them knew the way.

Neither of them knows the way, do **they**?

They bought **some** honey. (affirmative verb)

Did **some** of you sleep on the floor? (the answer 'yes' is expected)

Could you do **some** typing for me? (offer and request)

I have hardly **any** spare time. (negative verb or sentence)

He crossed the frontier without **any** difficulty.

Did he catch **any** fish? (question)

None of the tourists wants to climb the mountain.

We expected letters, but **none**(no letters) came.

Some idiot parked his car outside my garage. (an unspecified or unknown)

Any book about riding will tell you how to saddle a horse. (practically every)

EXERCISE

I. Choose the correct form that would be acceptable in each sentence.

1. I was delighted (hearing / to hear) the news.
2. (Serving / Served) in the army, he learned a great deal about electricity.
3. Three-fourths of the goods (making / made) in this factory are exported.
4. It was such (shocking / shocked) news that we couldn't believe it.
5. Those people who attended seemed very (interested / interesting).
6. Please don't forget to keep all the doors (locked / locking).
7. He refuses to do (anything dangerous / dangerous anything).
8. Crabs eat coconut, fish eat (alive / living) coral, and rat live in the tops of tall trees.
9. The salad tasted so (well / good) that my brother returned to the salad bar for another helping.
10. If it receives enough rain at the proper time, hay will grow quickly (like / as) grass.
11. Five minutes with a bright student may be equal (at / to) an hour with a slow one.
12. It is important to keep your supervisor (informative / informed) about any problems.
13. Background music has an (appreciable / appreciative) effect on employee productivity.
14. They all knew that the days (forward / ahead) would be tiresome.[2]

2 forward, backward는 '방향'을, ahead, behind는 '상태'를 나타냄.

15. There is an opening for an (experiencing / experienced) manager.

Ⅱ. Find an error in the underlined parts of each sentence and correct it.

1. There will be a twenty-minutes intermission between each session.

2. In modern industrious areas, sociocultural change is occurring at an accelerated rate.

3. Most great artists are exceptionally sensory people.

4. I had to think long and hardly before I could find the answer.

5. Although the quantity was small, we had supplies enough to finish the experiment.

6. Book keeping is limited to dealing with business having finance aspects.

7. It was hardly surprising that Barker felt wonderfully after pitching only the thirteenth perfect game in major league history.

8. If children were fed nourishing breakfasts before they left for school, there would be less problems in the early morning classes.

9. By the four year of an American President's administration the public has usually changed its perception of the man.

10. One of the outstanding characteristics of modern industrial society is its large degree of economic dependence upon mineral resources.

11. His highly imaginary composition won the judges' approval and the first prize in the high school essay contest.

12. There is no doubt in my mind that most important car of this year is the Metro Ⅳ.

13. I regret having to tell you that I'll have to be away from the office for the two first days next week.

Ⅲ. Choose the best completion for the following.

1. During the speech, he was half ____________ and wasn't able to listen to the speaker.

   a. sleep　　b. sleepy

   c. sleeping　　d. asleep

2. They are going to visit those stores for ____________ days of next week.

   a. first the three　　b. the three first

   c. the first three　　d. three the first

3. You will find that it is ____________ argument.

   a. a greatly exaggerated　　b. greatly an exaggerated

   c. an exaggerated greatly　　d. exaggerated a greatly

4. I ____________ awake past midnight.

   a. hardly ever stay　　b. hardly stay ever

   c. stay hardly ever　　d. stay ever hardly

5. This old desk isn't ____________ to sell, but maybe we could give it to someone.

   a. goodly enough　　b. good enough

   c. good as enough　　d. enough good

6. It is prohibited by law to mail through parcel post any merchandise that might prove __________ in transport.

a. dangerous | b. with danger
c. dangerously | d. to the danger

7. I happened to meet __________ English gentlemen in the lounge of the hotel.

a. two these fine good-natured old
b. these two old fine good-natured
c. these two fine good-natured old
d. old good-natured fine two these

8. There are still __________ obstacles to overcome in our way toward the eternal peace.

a. a lot | b. a great deal of
c. a great number of | d. many a

9. Workers in general are much less __________ to detail during the day if they haven't had sufficient rest.

a. attentively | b. attention
c. attentiveness | d. attentive

10. Because his response to the questions was less than __________, the school officials decided to deny him acceptance into their graduate program.

a. satisfaction | b. satisfied
c. satisfactory | d. satisfying

11. The company decided that a __________ more aggressive approach to advertising was needed to pull ahead of the competition.

a. so | b. very | c. much | d. really

12. This university's programs ____________ those of Harvard.

a. come second after
b. are second only to
c. are first except for
d. are in second place from

13. A: I think he is very wise.

B: No, he is ____________ than wise.

a. kinder
b. more kindly
c. more kind
d. so kind

4 부사(Adverb)

(1) 형용사와 부사의 의미를 모두 가지는 경우

(-ly의 부사형은 다른 뜻을 나타내기도 한다)

	형용사	부사	부사형	
fair	공정한	공정히	fairly	상당히
hard	어려운	열심히	hardly	거의 ~않는
high	높은	높이	highly	높게, 상당히
late	늦은	늦게	lately	최근에
most	대부분	가장	mostly	대개
near	가까운	가까이	nearly	거의
short	짧은	짧게	shortly	즉시
close	가까운	가까이	closely	면밀하게
great	훌륭한, 큰	훌륭히, 잘	greatly	매우
low	낮은	낮게	lowly	비천한, 겸손한, 신분이 낮은

I think **highly** of our company's founder.

Her work has piled up **high** on her desk.

In spite of a lack of practice, her writing has **greatly** improved.

Everything is going **great**.

My co-workers are **mostly** energetic and bright young people.

We **hardly** have enough time for lunch.

I was **nearly** finished my work when he came in.

I didn't have much contact with him ***lately***.

He worked overtime and came home ***late***.

She is a ***fast*** typist.

She can type ***fast***.

(2) 기타 형용사와 부사의 뜻을 모두 가지는 경우

	형용사	부사
daily	일상의	매일
fast	빠른	빨리
yearly	매년의	해마다
early	이른	일찍
long	긴	오래
enough	충분한	충분히
far	먼	멀리
pretty	예쁜	꽤, 아주

(3) 부사는 동사, 형용사, 다른 부사를 수식할 수 있다.

① 부사가 동사를 수식할 때는 본동사 앞 또는 be동사, 조동사 뒤에 위치한다.
그러나 때로는 본동사 뒤에서 수식할 때도 있다.
준동사와 목적어가 연속해 있을 때는 목적어 뒤에 오기도 한다.

Mr. Johnson **promptly** informed his supervisor of the accident.

Expense accounts for salesmen have been cut **substantially**.

It is necessary to filter each customer complaint **individually**.

His retirement has been **indefinitely** postponed.

They are **still** arranging the office to accommodate the new workers.

② 부사는 형용사, 또 다른 부사, 기타 수식어구를 수식한다.

Whether or not you quit is **entirely** up to you.

The service operates **only** on the dates listed below.

It may be **technically** impossible to lay the foundation for the memorial on the suggested site.

He gave an **exceptionally** profound speech at the gathering.

This picture has been **very** much admired.

(4) as ~ as 비교구문에서 형용사와 부사는 as ~ as 사이에 원급으로 온다.

My computer was as **slow** as a snail.

You'd better eat as **slowly** as possible.

It is not as **easy** as you think.

He is not as **young** as he used to be.

Take as **much** as you want.

(5) nearly, almost, just, very는 원급을, much, even, still, far, a lot, by far는 비교급을, much, by far, quite, the very, only는 최상급을 강조한다.

She is **just** as intelligent and good-looking as he.

He is **by far** the most forceful of all the speakers at the convention.

There is a **much** better store around the corner.

(6) quite의 쓰임

① **'a, an+명사' 앞에서 강조**

The new archiving system was **quite a success**.

② **'not quite'로 "완전히 ~는 아니다"의 뜻**

I'm **not quite** ready to take the next step.

③ **quite가 동사, 형용사, 부사 등을 강조할 때는 '매우, 상당히, 꽤'를 의미**

The performance was **quite** surprising.

(7) so, such, too

① **so**는 부사로서 형용사나 부사를 수식하지만 **such**는 형용사로서 명사를 수식한다.

The store was **so busy** that it had to hire additional part-time workers.

Sales items sold out **so quickly** that the shop had to close early.

He had never dealt with **such an experienced negotiator** before.

> cf) It's amazing that one company can have so(such) dedicated employees.
>
> so: 대단히 헌신적인 직원들
> such: 그토록 헌신적인 직원들

② **too**는 '너무 ~하다'의 뜻으로 형용사를 꾸미지만 부사를 꾸며줄 때도 있다.

This is too complicated for the students to understand.

They had eaten too much food to go jogging in the park.

This study is much too comprehensive for him to handle.

They ate the food too much.

(8) later, thereafter

① **later: ~후에, 나중에**

He was questioned about the scandal five months later. (5개월 후에)

Why don't we talk this over later? (나중에)

② **thereafter: 그 이후에**

Mary left and her package was delivered shortly thereafter. (그 이후에 바로)

(9) already, still, yet

① **already: '이미, 벌써' (긍정문)**

She has **already** typed the report you left.

② **still: '아직, 여전히' (부정문, 긍정문, 의문문)**

The house is **still** up for sale.

③ **yet: '아직(도)' (부정문, 긍정문), '이미, 벌써' (의문문)**

Have you finished your breakfast **yet**?

Much **yet** remains to be done.

Haven't you been there **yet**?

EXERCISE

I. Choose the correct form that would be acceptable in each sentence.

1. The (highly / high) successful book launch was attended by thousands of people.
2. Whether or not you quit is (entire / entirely) up to you.
3. Sales of compact disc players have gone down (nearly / near) 20 percent this year.
4. The funds for the event are (still / yet) not sufficient.
5. He hadn't even started the project (still / yet).
6. The staff was (so / such) argumentative that it took time before decisions were made.
7. Cocoa is exported (wide / widely) to nearly every part of world.
8. The actual annual report figures came (close / closely) to this year's production estimates.
9. Investors want the company to be (sufficiently / sufficient) strong before they consider putting money into it.
10. Acting as the vice president of (such / so) a large company was (such / so) stressful that she retired early.
11. They prepared (much too / too much) food, believing that many people would be participating.
12. You are (certain / certainly) one of the most persuasive salespeople we have met.

II. Find an error in the underlined parts of each sentence and correct it.

1. Dresses, skirts, shoes, and children's clothing are advertised at great reduced prices this weekend.

2. John always arrives lately for his chemistry class even though he leaves his dormitory in plenty of time.

3. That product that you bought at the lower price is the more inferior to the one that we sell at the slightly higher price.

4. Morale among the staff has been raised substantial by the new esprosso machine in the lounge.

5. The discovery of X-rays in 1895 by W.C. Roentgen was pure accidental.

6. Because the residents had worked so diligent to renovate the old building, the manager had a party.

7. She was noticeably upset by how indignant he responded to her final question.

8. That novel is definitely a dense-packed narrative, which requires a vast knowledge of cultural background or an excellent encyclopedia.

9. The children were playing last night outdoors, when it began to rain very hard.

10. Despite the time of the year, yesterday's temperature was enough hot to turn on the air conditioning.

11. George has not completed the assignment yet, and Maria hasn't so.

12. In order for one to achieve the desired results in this experiment it is necessary that he work as fastly as possible.

13. Several people have apparent tried to change the man's mind, but he refuses to listen.

14. Since the 1930s, air transport has brought about a revolution as great as that of the railways a century ago.

Ⅲ. Choose the best completion for the following.

1. She was fired ____________ after getting into a heated debate with the manager about appropriate office etiquette.

   a. shortly b. shorter c. short d. shorten

2. Last year, Matt earned ____________ his brother, who has a better position.

   a. twice as much as b. twice as many as
   c. twice more than d. twice as more as

3. Of all the students in the class, Jane is ____________.

   a. very taller than all her classmates
   b. the tallest of all the girls
   c. taller than any girl
   d. by far the tallest

4. Peter enjoys going to concerts ____________.

   a. in a while b. at occasion
   c. at sometimes d. from time to time

5. Sara didn't go to visit her aunt ______________.

a. the last week
b. the week before
c. this past week
d. a week past

6. ______________, the man smoked with moody composure.

a. From an out view
b. Outwardly
c. On the outside
d. Out

7. ______________, he is misunderstood by most people.

a. By large
b. On the whole
c. Wholly
d. Largely

8. The store that had ______________ went bankrupt.

a. the big sale recently
b. the big recently sale
c. the recently big sale
d. recently the big sale

9. I have paid for so many traffic violations that I ______________ a regular customer.

a. almost become
b. almost have become
c. have almost become
d. have almost to become

10. Cactus stems remains moist and juicy ______________ plants become dry.

a. and other long after
b. other after long
c. after other long and
d. long after other

11. The manufacturer sells to the wholesalers and wholesalers sell to the stores at ______________ price.

a. a higher slightly
b. a slightly higher
c. slightly a higher
d. higher a slightly

12. She has lived in this house since 1980; that is to say, ______________ since her father died.

a. very
b. ever
c. such
d. as

5 대명사(Pronoun)

(1) 'It'의 용법

① **비인칭 주어 it:**

날씨, 시간, 명암, 거리, 불특정 상황 등을 나타낼 때 해석하지 않는 형식적인 주어로 사용한다.

It is very sunny day.

It is half past seven.

It's still dark outside.

It is twenty minutes' walk from here to the office.

How is it with your children?

② **가주어, 가목적어 it:**

형식적으로 주어나 목적어 자리에 나타나지만 해석하지 않는다.

가주어(it)… 진주어(to, ~ing, that)…

It is quite natural **that he should be upset**.

Isn't **it** a shame **that they lost the game**?

It is very important **to exercise regularly**.

It is impolite **to smoke in public places**.

It is difficult **learning a foreign language**.

가목적어(it)… 진목적어(to, ~ing, that)…

I think **it** natural **that he should pass the examination**.

I believe **it** bad **to eat much food at night**.

We found **it** interesting **learning new sports.**

John kept **it** a secret **that he helped the poor**.

Tim made **it** a rule never **to watch television on Sunday**.

③ **It ~ that 강조구문:**

It와 that절 사이에 강조하고자 하는 부분을 넣어 표현할 수 있다.

It was **at the theater** that the couple went on their first date.

It was **not until yesterday** that they arrested all thieves in this town.

It is **his friends** that(who) helped him stop drinking.

cf) **It** is my opinion **that government should not raise taxes again**.
가주어 / 진주어

(2) It가 포함된 관용적인 표현

At last, we've **made it**. (결국 우리가 해냈다)

I will **give it** him **hot**. (혼내 주겠다, 따끔한 맛을 보여주겠다)

You must **make a clean breast of it**. (모든 것을 솔직하게 털어놓아야 한다)

That's **the way it is**. (사는 것이 그렇지 뭐)

Go for it. (힘 내)

Take it easy. (천천히 해, 잘 지내)

I **couldn't help it**. (어쩔 수 없었어)

I **got it**. (알았어)

If you **give it a try**, you'll probably like **it**. (한 번 해 보면 좋아할 거야)

(3) 재귀대명사 용법

① 동일한 한 문장 내에서 앞의 명사 자체를 나타낼 때 사용한다.

She prides **herself** on her achievement. (자랑스럽게 여기다)

He has to shave **himself** twice a day. (면도하다)

She cried **herself** to sleep. (울다가 잠들었다)

He devoted **himself** to always improving his performance. (전념하다)

② 명사나 대명사를 강조할 때 쓰인다.

I **myself** have never been there.

The plan was simplicity **itself**.

Mr. York unexpectedly completed the forms **himself**.

③ 여러 인칭이 혼합되어 쓰일 때 1인칭이 포함되어 있으면 ourselves, 1인칭이 없고 2인칭이 포함되면 yourselves로 표현한다.

You, John, and I must not deceive **ourselves**.

You and John must not lie about **yourselves**.

④ 관용적인 표현으로 사용하는 재귀대명사

by oneself (=alone): 혼자서

for oneself (=without other help): 혼자 힘으로

of oneself (=naturally): 저절로

beside oneself (=out of one's senses): 제 정신이 아닌

in itself (=in its own nature): 본질적으로, 그 자체로

in spite of oneself (=unconsciously): 자신도 모르게

to oneself (=not shared by anyone else): 혼자서만, 독점하여

between ourselves: 우리끼리 얘기지만

enjoy oneself: 마음껏 즐기다

behave oneself: 점잖게 행동하다

absent oneself (from): 결석하다

avail oneself (of): 이용하다

help oneself to N: ~을 마음껏 먹다

seat oneself: 앉다

dress oneself: 치장하다

say to oneself: 혼잣말하다

make oneself at home: 편안해하다

make oneself understood: 의사소통하다

(4) 부정대명사

① one, some, any

❶ 앞에서 말한 명사와 같은 종류이지만 불특정한 다른 대상을 나타낼 때 쓰인다.

A: Do you have **a laptop**?

B: Yes, I have **one**. But it doesn't work well, so I want to buy a new **one**.

❷ 앞에서 말한 명사가 복수일 때는 ones를 사용한다.

He has ten dogs, and I have five **ones**.

My sister has two big dolls and four small **ones**.

He bought her a red hairpin, but she wanted a white **one**.

cf) He lost **his foreign stamps**, but he found **them** in his room.
⇒ 앞에서 언급한 명사 자체를 수식할 때는 대명사를 사용한다.

② some, any

Do you have *anything* new to tell me?

I haven't *anything* useful to give you.

Can I ask you *something*?

Some of our best employees are here today.

Anybody you recommend will be welcomed.

There is coffee in the lounge if you want *any*.

If *anybody* phones for me while I'm out, tell him I'll call back later.

> cf) He left town on *some* pressing business
> I doubt if such a thing is of *any* practical use.

③ none

앞에서 언급한 명사를 부정할 때 사용하며 가산명사와 불가산명사에 모두 쓰인다. 일반적으로 단수로 취급하지만 복수로 취급하는 경우도 있다.

He asked for some documentary **proof** but I had **none**.

None of the sailors was experienced (formal)

None of the people were happy. (informal)

None of the information was correct.

④ -one, -thing, -body, etc.

someone, anyone, anybody, everyone, everybody, no one, something, anything, everything, nothing 등은 항상 단수 취급한다.

There **was** no one at the office when I arrived.

Everybody **knows** about the secret.

Nobody **leaves** the room without permission.

Almost anything **goes** these days

Someone **wants** to speak to you on the phone.

Nobody **has** ever given me a free ticket for anything.

Do you want anything from the chemist?

Someone's passport has been stolen.

Is this somebody's/anybody's seat?

I don't want to waste anyone's time.

Has anyone left their luggage on the train?

Something went wrong, didn't it?

cf) If **anybody** phones for me while I'm out, tell **them** I'll phone **them** back later on.

⇒ 구어체에서 부정대명사를 they나 them으로 받는 경우도 있다.

⑤ **each, every**

❶ each는 단독 또는 단수명사와 함께 쓰이며 단수동사를 취한다. 단, each of 뒤에는 복수명사를 취한다.

Each **has** its own value.

Each person **has** a different voice.

Each of them **doesn't** have enough time to sleep.

❷ every는 단수명사와 함께 쓰이며 단수동사를 갖는다.

Every soccer player was issued a new uniform.

cf) each, every가 부사로 쓰일 때도 있다.

She sells computers 300 dollars **each**. (각각)

This bus comes **every** ten minutes. (~마다)

(5) another, other 활용용법

① **another:**

많은 대상 중에서 '또 다른 하나(한 사람), 또는 하나 더'를 뜻하며 대체로 가산명사의 단수형 앞에 쓰인다. 단, 숫자를 동반한 복수명사 앞에 쓰일 수 있다. another 앞에는 관사나 다른 한정어가 쓰이지 않는다.

They opened **another store** last month.

I hope to stay **another five days** in this city.

Can you show me **another route**?

We need to review **another two reports** on this matter.

② **other:**

other는 확정적이지 않은 영역에 있는 것을 가리키는 '다른~'의 뜻을 가지며 복수형 명사와 함께 쓰이거나 자체를 복수형으로 쓸 수 있다.

I can't speak any **other foreign languages**.

Be kind to **others**.

Our team has **one** member from England and **others** from Germany and Japan.

③ **the other(s):**

제한된 영역 내에서 일부를 제외한 나머지 모두를 가리킬 때는 the others를, 비교 대상이 둘 일 때 다른 하나를 나타낼 때는 the other를 쓴다.

Many people were invited, but **some** accepted and **the others** refused.

She carried a case in **one** hand and an umbrella in **the other**.

Some tourists went on the beach; **others** explored the town.

④ **the one… the other…:**

문장에서 언급한 내용의 전자와 후자를 가리킨다.

Health is better than wealth; **the one** gives us more happiness than **the other**.

⑤ **one… another:**

셋 이상의 사물이나 사람에 대해 언급할 때 '하나는 ~ 다른 하나는 ~이다'를 뜻한다.

She hung her hat on **one** hook and her raincoat on **another**.

The topic of their conversation skipped from **one** to **another**.

One student suggested a play, **another** student wanted a concert.

⑥ **ⓐ is one thing, ⓑ is another: ⓐ와 ⓑ는 별개다.**

Saying **is one thing**, and doing **is another**.

(6) 기타 양화사와 관련한 대명사

All of the passengers ***are*** on board.

Most of the luggage ***is*** now on board.

All of the money ***was*** from America.

Half of the food ***has*** been eaten.

Half of the people ***have*** been there.

Fifty percent of the food ***has*** been eaten.

Fifty percent of the books ***were*** stolen.

The rest of the food ***has*** spoiled.

The rest of the sandwiches ***are*** in the kitchen.

The majority of the population ***was*** very young.

The majority of the people ***were*** financed by the foundation.

EXERCISE

I. Choose the correct form that would be acceptable in each sentence.

1. His smart phone is very wonderful, and I bought the same (one / it).
2. Susan has five dresses. One is white, (another / the second) is bluish green, and (the others / others) are red.
3. The family has two houses; one is in Korea and (the other / another) is in Hawaii.
4. There were many victims by the earthquake; some are adults, (the others / others) are children.
5. People at the party are shaking hands and greeting (one another / each other).
6. Each of students (is / are) good at speaking English.
7. (All the coins / All of coins) on the desk are made of nickel and copper.
8. (We both / Both of us / Both we) like Korean food more than Japanese food.
9. You have to pay extra for the cab if you have (some baggage / some baggages).
10. These trousers seem to become you better than the other (one / ones).
11. The brakes are useless and (that is / those are) why the car needs to go into the garage.
12. I cut (mine / myself) when I was opening a can, but it's not serious.
13. We met the Smith family in the hotel; they had the room next to (ours / us).

II. Find an error in the underlined parts of each sentence and correct it.

1. All of the furnitures that Mary bought last month was made in Sweden.

2. While John was carrying the paint can from the garage to the house, some of it spilled on his pants.

3. Each cigarette which a person smokes does some harm, and eventually he may get a serious disease from their effects.

4. It was him who came running into the classroom with the news.

5. It was until almost thirty years after his death that a plaque in memory of Dylan Thomas was placed in Westminster Abbey.

6. In the name of science, the eighteenth century explorer, Alexander Von Humboldt, defied death by deliberately risking electrocuting him with an electric eel.

7. Some bumper stickers are very funny and make us laugh, yet another can make us angry because of their ridiculousness.

8. The president refuses to accept either of the four new proposals made by the contractors.

9. There are usually a lot of traffic in the city at this time of the day.

10. I've tried all the morning to reserve a room but none the hotels have any vacancies.

11. Our service we offer is helping people fill out tax forms and send it to the authorities.

12. Advertising agencies help companies sell its products or services.

13. Bill is the only one in the office at the moment. Everyone else have gone home.

14. Managers may need to summarize long and complex policies, and then convey it to the employees.

15. We are going to send out the application form to whomever asks for it in time.

Ⅲ. Choose the best completion for the following.

1. ______________ the Christmas shopping season begins.

   a. That is after Thanksgiving b. After Thanksgiving it is

   c. It is after Thanksgiving that d. It is Thanksgiving that

2. ______________ the windchill factor which gives the best idea of how a person will feel outside on a cold day.

   a. It is b. There is

   c. It was d. There was

3. I saw ______________ at the barber's.

   a. my sister's boyfriend b. a boyfriend of my sister

   c. my sister of boyfriend d. a boyfriend of my sister's

4. You had better set off early to give ______________ plenty of time to get there.

   a. your b. yourself

   c. yours d. you

5. Manufacturers may make their products far from the places where customers buy ______________.

a. it　　b. one　　c. them　　d. ones

6. It was their fault, not ______________, that they hadn't checked the companies credit status.

a. us　　b. ours　　c. we　　d. our

7. He wrote some books for children but ______________ for adults.

a. no　　b. some

c. any　　d. none

8. He blamed ______________ for not paying attention, but the accident wasn't his fault.

a. his　　b. him

c. he　　d. himself

9. She decorated the whole house, inside and outside, ______________ her own.

a. on　　b. at

c. by　　d. with

10. Half of my colleagues work in sales and ______________ half work in marketing.

a. another　　b. the other

c. others　　d. one

11. We began a unique real-estate development business and it is different from ______________.

a. theirs　　b. them

c. they　　d. their

12. Nancy does ____________ on Friday, so the weekend is free for the family.

a. every housework
b. every houseworks
c. all the housework
d. all the houseworks

13. I've been to two or three of her parties before, but not ____________.

a. all them
b. they all
c. all they
d. all of them

14. In the morning, Helen spends ____________ of her time making phone calls.

a. most
b. a few
c. many
d. every

6 관계사(Relatives)

[1] 관계대명사(Relative Pronoun)

둘 이상의 절을 주절과 종속절을 가진 하나의 절로 연결시키는 관계대명사는 선행사와 격에 따라 달리 사용된다.

선행사		사람	사물, 동물	사람, 사물	
격	주격	who	which	that	what
	목적격	whom	which	that	what
	소유격	whose	whose of which	-	-

Did you get the package? The package came in the mail.

→ Did you get the package **that** came in the mail?

Archaeologists have explored many sites. Their ruins have deteriorated.

→ Archaeologists have explored many sites **whose** ruins have deteriorated.

(1) 주격관계대명사:

일반적으로 생략할 수 없지만 be동사가 뒤따를 때는 그 be동사와 함께 생략할 수 있다. 완료시제를 가질 때도 축약 가능하다.

The man **who/that** found the ruins was named Stephens.

We have to leave now to catch the train **which/that** leaves at five.

He keeps a dog **which/that** barks fiercely.

Machu Picchu **(which is)** located high in the Andes was constructed by the Incas.

South America has many areas **(which are)** filled with archaeological wonders.

The temples **(that were)** being built during this time had a variety of designs.

The Taj Mahal, **(which was)** built by Shah Jahan, is made of white marble.

The workers, **who had finally finished the temple**, returned to their villages.
= The workers, **finally having finished the temple**, returned to their villages.

The workers **who had not been paid** refused to continue on the project.
= The workers **not having been paid** refused to continue on the project.

(2) 목적격관계대명사:

생략할 수 있지만 전치사가 관계대명사 앞에 쓰일 때는 생략할 수 없다.

Have you arranged the schedule **(which/that)** I need for today?

Do you know the woman **(whom)** Helen is talking with?

(Do you know the woman **with whom** Helen is talking?)

This is the office **in which** they work.

This is a boy **(whom)** you can absolutely depend on.

(3) 소유격관계대명사: 생략할 수 없다.

I have a friend **whose** father runs a business in LA.
(I have a friend. His father runs a business in LA.)

The woman **whose** daughter you met is Mrs. Brown.
(The woman is Mrs. Brown. You met her daughter.)

Kings employed priests **whose** job was to keep written records.
(Kings employed priests. Their job was to keep written records.)

The Mayans had a well-organized society **whose** kings had absolute power.
(The Mayans had a well-organized society. The Mayans' kings had absolute power.)

(4) that 용법

① 선행사가 사람과 사물이 함께 나타날 때 쓴다.

This is a story about a man and his dog **that** lived in the cave.

② 선행사가 의문사(who, which, what), 서수, 최상급, the very, the only, all, the same, no, any, every, ~thing, ~body 등 일 때는 that만을 쓴다.

Who that has common sense will do such a thing?

This is **the first** letter **that** came from Japan.

This is **the most interesting** book **that** I have ever read.

Nobody that knows him will believe him.

You are **the only** one **that** can solve this problem.

The very fact **that** he returned safely is a miracle.

He didn't say **anything that** wasn't true

She reads **the same** books **that** you do.

③ 관계대명사 앞에 전치사가 쓰일 때는 that을 쓰지 못한다.

This is the university **that** he works **at**.

This is the university **at which** he works.

④ that은 계속적인 용법으로 쓰지 않는다.

The figure**, that** I like the most, is of a horse. (×)

The figure **that** I like the most is of a horse. (○)

⑤ 관계절에 be동사가 있고 관계대명사가 관계절의 보어로 쓰일 때 that을 쓴다.

He is not the man **that** he was. (그는 과거의 그가 아니다)

My typewriter is not the machine **that** it was.
(내 타자기는 이전의 그 타자기가 아니다)

(5) 복합관계대명사

복합관계대명사	명사절	부사절
whoever	anyone who (~하는 누구든지)	no matter who (누가 ~하더라도)
whatever	anything that (~하는 것은 무엇이든지)	no matter what (무엇을 ~하더라도)
whichever	anything which (~하는 어느 것이든지)	no matter which (어떤 것을 ~하더라도)

◆ 부사절:

Whichever bus you take, it'll pass by Seoul Station.
(No matter which bus you take, ~)
(어떤 버스를 타더라도 서울역을 지나간다)

I don't want to see them, **whoever** they are. (~, no matter who they are.)
(그들이 누구라도 나는 그들을 만나고 싶지 않다)

He looks gorgeous, **whatever** he wears. (~, no matter what he wears.)
(무엇을 입더라도 그는 멋져 보인다)

◆ 명사절:

You can have **whichever** you like. (You can have anything which you like.)
(네가 좋아하는 것이면 어떤 것이든지 가질 수 있다)

Whoever breaks this law shall be punished. (Anyone who breaks this law~)
(이 법을 어기는 사람은 누구든지 처벌받을 것이다)

Take **whatever** action is needed. (Take anything that action is needed.)
(필요한 조치는 무엇이든지 취하라)

(6) 계속적인 용법과 한정적인 용법

① 계속적인 용법

This is Easter Island, **where** an advanced society had flourished.

This is Easter Island, **on which** an advanced society had flourished.

This is Easter Island, **which** an advanced society had flourished **on**.

This is Easter Island, **that** an advanced society had flourished **on**. (incorrect)

This is Easter Island, an advanced society had flourished **on**. (incorrect)

② 한정적인 용법

This is an island **where** an advanced society had flourished.

This is an island **on which** an advanced society had flourished.

This is an island **which** an advanced society had flourished **on**.

This is an island **that** an advanced society had flourished **on**.

This is an island an advanced society had flourished **on**.

(7) 수량을 나타내는 한정어와 함께 쓰는 관계대명사

Sailors attacked the islanders, **three of whom** were killed.

These statues, **many of which** weigh over 20 tons, are world famous.

They sailed two ships, **neither of which** was safe.

A few sculptures, **one of which** was over 70 feet long, were left in the rock quarry.

(8) 선행사와 관계대명사절 동사의 수 일치

The **islanders** who **were** kidnapped later died.

It was **the only one** of the islands that **was** formed by volcanoes.

It is one of **the islands** that **were** formed by volcanoes.

[2] 관계부사(Relative Adverb)

(1) 때, 장소, 이유, 방법 등의 부사

때, 장소, 이유, 방법 등 부사의 특징을 나타내는 선행사가 있을 때 각각 관계부사 when, where, why, how가 쓰인다.

The school **where** I teach is going to hire more teachers.
Do you remember the time **when** Mrs. Barnes phoned me?
Can you tell me **why** Paul was transferred to Ottawa?
The record shows **how** the company expanded its overseas branches.

선행사	관계부사	전치사+관계대명사
시간(day, year, time)	when	at/in/on which
장소(place, area)	where	at/in/on which
이유(the reason)	why	for which
방법(the way)	how	in which

cf) 1. when은 생략 가능하나 선행사와 떨어져 있을 때는 생략할 수 없다.

That was the second time (when) we met.
The time will come **when** you will regret it.

2. 선행사가 생략되면 관계절이 명사절이 된다.

He remembers when there was no electric light.

(2) 복합관계부사

복합관계부사	시간·장소 부사절	양보 부사절
whenever	at any time when (~하는 언제든지)	no matter when (언제 ~하더라도)
wherever	at any place where (~하는 어디든지)	no matter where (어디에서 ~하더라도)
however		no matter how (아무리 ~하더라도)

You can ask for help **whenever you need it**.
(=at any time when, 필요할 때면 언제든지)

She has the window open **however cold it is outside**.
(=no matter how, 바깥이 아무리 춥더라도)

The famous politician gathers a crowd easily **wherever he goes**.
(=no matter where, 그가 어디를 가더라도)

Paul met his fans **wherever he visited**.
(=at any place where, 그가 방문했던 어디든지)

Lots of people came to see Steve Jobs **whenever he made a presentation.**
(=no matter when, 그가 언제 발표를 하더라도(발표할 때면 언제나))

EXERCISE

Ⅰ. Choose the correct form that would be acceptable in each sentence.

1. Erich von Daniken is one of the scientists who (has / have) proposed theories about Easter Island's statues.
2. Von Daniken's book *Chariots of the Gods* is one of a few books that (suggest / suggests) that extraterrestrials built the statues.
3. Machu Picchu, which is (located / locating) high in the Andes, was constructed by the Incas.
4. The god (that / who) the Athenians saw as their protector was Athena.
5. The Parthenon, (which / that) tourists visit daily, must be protected.
6. Here is the article about (which / what) I was speaking.
7. The only thing left to consider is (which / how) we invest the money.
8. Inside the gallery is a small bookstore (where / which) you can buy prints and postcards.
9. Summer is the time (at which / which) accidental water injuries occur most often.
10. The technician patiently showed me (how / why) I could install the new software on my computer.
11. You should not forget to take off your shoes (wherever / whenever) you enter someone's house.
12. Could I speak to (whoever / whomever) is in charge of the Marketing Department?
13. He gave me a lot of advice, much of (them / which) was very useful.

14. Is that the boy (whom / who) you spoke of the other day?

15. I have already written to Mr. Harris, (who / which) will no doubt be contacting you in the near future.

Ⅱ. Find an error in the underlined parts of each sentence and correct it.

1. A variety of economic indicators, some of which is the consumer price index, are used to calculate the rate of inflation.

2. This is Easter Island, where an advanced society had flourished here.

3. Cézanne was one of the painters who was part of the 1874 exhibition that would mark the beginnings of impressionism.

4. I know I can count on you no matter whenever I need your support, which is a great comfort for me.

5. The prize is given to firms whom programs contribute to the community.

6. It's produced by a cell phone manufacturer with who we have business ties.

7. In any place wherever she goes, there are crowds of people waiting to see her.

8. This is the place where I have long wanted to visit.

9. That Mr. Johnson started his publishing career is 1942 whenever he founded the Johnson Publishing Company in Chicago.

10. Before I die, I feel it my duty to pass on to you such wisdom which I have acquired.

11. He is the only candidate who the faculty members voted not to retain on the list of eligible replacements for Professor Kotey.

12. There are many organizations which sole purpose is to help mentally retarded children.

Ⅲ. Choose the best completion for the following.

1. Today, the Egyptian pyramids are endangered by pollution, __________ may destroy them completely.

   a. the effect of it　　b. whose its effect
   c. whose effect　　d. which its effect

2. Dr. John, __________ at the party, will teach History 225 next semester.

   a. who we met her　　b. whom we met
   c. whom we met her　　d. we met

3. It took skilled craftsmen __________ day and night for 22 years to build the Taj Mahal.

   a. who working　　b. worked
   c. who they were working　　d. working

4. Ancient craftsmen, __________, made and painted this pottery.

   a. about whom little is known　　b. about who little is known
   c. who little is known　　d. little is known about whom

5. We apply a laboratory test to every product we make, which is __________ it is so reliable.

   a. that　　b. why　　c. what　　d. in which

6. The manager prefers to interview candidates ____________ resumes are well written.

a. which
b. whom
c. whose
d. that

7. The manufacturing company ____________ Mr. Dice works has hired over two hundred employees over the past two months.

a. when
b. which
c. where
d. what

8. Mr. Duncan, ____________ firm lost a lot of money, called for more bonus for himself.

a. which
b. whose
c. whom
d. that

9. We all should remember ____________ the director said when he left the company.

a. when
b. which
c. that
d. what

10. It was he ____________ we thought would win the prize.

a. who
b. whom
c. whose
d. whoever

11. He had no friend ____________ whom he could talk about the matter.

a. for
b. in
c. with
d. of

12. We're going to take a holiday in September, ____________ the weather isn't so hot.

a. when
b. where
c. that
d. which

13. She changed her mind again, ____________ made us all angry.

a. who
b. which
c. whom
d. that

14. Most of ______________ now Louisiana was once part of an ancient bay of the Gulf of Mexico.

a. what is
b. it is
c. what is it
d. what it is

15. A marsupial is an animal ______________ babies are raised in a pouch in the mother's body.

a. is
b. who its
c. that
d. whose

16. Jane was an early twentieth-century actress ______________ the most beautiful woman on the American stage.

a. was called by critics
b. critics called her
c. whom critics called
d. whom critics called her

17. A bone marrow test, ______________ involves extracting fluid from the marrow, may be necessary for diagnosing leukemia.

a. what
b. which
c. that
d. in which

18. The senator depended upon ______________.

a. Whomever was willing to assist him
b. whoever will assist him
c. whoever he wanted to assist
d. whoever was willing to assist him

7 To 부정사(To-infinitive)

(1) 부정사의 용법

① 명사적 용법:

부정사가 문장에서 주어, 목적어, 보어로 쓰인다.

To use the smart phone application is very useful. (주어)

We want **to end poverty all over the world**. (목적어)

Her plan is **to skip supper** every other day. (보어)

His ambition, **to be a leading actor**, was never fulfilled. (동격)

◈ **[의문사 + to부정사]** 구문도 명사적 특성을 갖는다.

He knows **how to drive** a car.

Please tell me **what to do**.

We didn't decide **when to leave** here.

Where to live is the most important problem.

→ [의문사 + 주어 + should + 동사원형]으로 바꾸어 쓸 수 있다.

We didn't decide when to leave here.
= We didn't decide when we should leave here.

② 형용사적 용법:

to부정사 바로 앞의 명사나 대명사를 꾸며주며 '~할'로 해석한다.

I am looking for an American **to teach** me English.

She couldn't keep her promise **to write** to me every weekend.

Sam wants something **to eat** now.

◈ **[be동사 + to부정사]**

예정: I **am to** interview the daily newsmen tomorrow.

The train **is to** arrive in five minutes.

의무: He **is to** stop smoking to live a healthy life.

You **are not to** put chalk marks on the fences.

가능: The report **was not to** be found in the newspaper.

My computer **was to** be repaired.

운명: He **was never to** see his homeland again.

They **were to** come back home again.

의도: If you **are** really **to** succeed in anything, you must make a good start.

If you **are to** be healthy, eat organic food.

③ **부사적 용법:**

❶ **동사수식**

ⓐ 목적: ~하기 위해서

She doesn't eat fatty food **to lose** weight.
(= She doesn't eat fatty food **in order to lose** weight.)
(= She doesn't eat fatty food **so as to lose** weight.)
(= She doesn't eat fatty food **so that she can lose** weight.)

He studied hard **not to fail** the exam.

I went to the book store **to buy** English books.

ⓑ 원인: ~해서, ~ 때문에

She was delighted **to win** a gold medal.

He was shocked **to hear** her vulgar expressions.

They were disappointed **to get** an F grade in math.

ⓒ 결과: ~해서 결과적으로 ~이다

The boy grew up **to be** a great scientist.

She woke suddenly **to find** someone standing in the doorway with a candle.

He raised our expectations only **to disappoint** us.

ⓓ 이유, 판단의 근거: ~하다니 ~일 것이다.

He must be crazy **to spend** so much time on puzzles.

He must be crazy **to talk** like that.

ⓔ 조건: ~이면, ~한다면

She may be disappointed **to note** that I got just three pieces of mail.

To tell the truth, the prospect isn't bright.

❷ **형용사 수식**

Korean is not *easy* **to learn**.

What is *good* **to eat** is good for you.

He is *tough* **to deal with**.

❸ **부사 수식**

She is old *enough* **to go** there alone.

Your question is *too* complicated **to answer** in two minutes.

Who is *so* wise *as* **to do** such a thing if not Ron?

(2) too~ to, enough to, so ~ as to

The animal runs **too** swiftly **to** catch.
(= The animal runs so swiftly that we cannot catch it.)

My budget was big **enough** for me **to** rent an apartment.
(= My budget was so big that I could rent an apartment.)

The star is **so** bright **as to** be seen with the naked eye.
(= The star is so bright that it can be seen with the naked eye.)

(3) 원형부정사

① 지각동사(see, look at, watch, hear, listen to, feel, smell)는 목적보어로 원형부정사를 갖는다.

I can see her **dance** on the stage.

I felt my dog **bite** my thumb.

I listened to her **talk** to a guest from beginning to end.

cf) 1. 동작이 진행 중임을 강조할 경우 목적보어로 현재 분사형(~ing)을 쓴다.

We could **see** him **running** fast.

We **watched** Thomas **hanging** on the horizontal bar.

2. 지각동사가 수동태인 경우 원형부정사 대신 to부정사를 쓴다.

A strange man **was seen to steal** Rachel's bag by me.
(= I **saw** a strange man **steal** Rachel's bag.)

② 사역동사(let, have, make)는 목적보어로 원형부정사를 쓴다.

Let me **get** a taxi for you.

John **let** them **use** his car.

They **made** each applicant **write** a personal essay.

I'll **have** my secretary **send** off the catalogs to you.

cf) 1. **get**은 사역동사이지만 목적보어로 to부정사를 갖는다.

I **got** the teller **to check** my savings account.

He **got** his son **to wash** his car.

2. **help**는 목적보어로 to부정사와 원형부정사 모두 쓸 수 있다.

My mother **helped** me **(to) do** my homework

③ 사역동사와 지각동사의 목적어가 '사물'인 경우 목적보어는 과거분사형이 된다.

I **heard** my name **mentioned**.

She **had** her hair **cut** short.

Henry **made** his pants **shortened**.

Cathy **had** her sister's bike **repaired** and **repainted** all red.

④ to부정사의 의미상주어

to부정사의 의미적 주어는 목적격으로 나타내며 그 의미상 주어 앞에 사람의 성질이나 태도를 나타내는 형용사가 나올 때는 의미상 주어 앞에 of를 쓴다. 그 외에는 for를 쓴다.

<사람의 성품이나 태도를 나타내는 형용사> *kind, brave, stupid, silly, careful, careless, nice, wise, honest, foolish, nice, dishonest, polite, impolite, cruel, generous, thoughtful, rude,* …

It is *generous* **of** him to forgive his enemy.

It is *thoughtful* **of** her to make way for an ambulance.

It was so *cruel* **of** him to do such a thing.

There is no *time* **for** you to crack a joke.

It is very *dangerous* **for** us to dive off the cliff.

It was *unbelievable* **for** Tim to get an F grade in literature.

(4) to부정사를 목적어로 취하는 동사:

agree, appear, arrange, be, be about, be supposed, afford, care, claim, come, consent, decide, demand, deserve, endeavor, fail, forget, happen, hesitate, hope, learn, manage, mean, offer, plan, prepare, pretend, proceed, prove, refuse, seem, serve, struggle, swear, tend, threaten, volunteer, wait, ask, dare, expect, beg, choose, intend, need, prefer, promise, wish, etc.

We **can't afford to** move now.

Do you **care to** have some coffee?

She **deserves to** be paid more.

I **failed to** recognize the problem.

He **pretended to** be sleeping.

She **refused to** help him.

I **volunteered to** help after school.

Everyone **agreed to** meet at the museum.

We **plan never to** go there on a holiday again.

We **waited to** say good-bye.

We **decided not to** leave early.

(5) 목적보어로 to부정사를 사용하는 동사:

allow, appoint, believe, cause, caution, challenge, command, compel, convince, direct, enable, encourage, forbid, force, get, hire, implore, instruct, motivate, oblige, order, permit, persuade, remind, require, teach, tell, urge, use, warn, etc.

I **hired** him **to** do the work.

We **told** him **to** finish the report.

It **enables** me **to** remember many things.

Don't **expect** him **to** quit smoking and drinking.

The doorman **allowed** us **to** enter the building.

(6) 부정사의 시제

① 단순부정사

❶ appear, seem, be said, be thought, be believed 등 뒤에 단순시제의 부정사가 오면 이들 동사와 부정사의 동작이나 상태가 같은 시제임을 뜻한다.

She *seems* **to be** happy.
(=It seems that she is happy.)

She *seemed* **to be** happy.
(=It seemed that she was happy.)

❷ want, hope, expect, wish 등 희망이나 기대를 나타내는 동사 뒤에 단순시제의 부정사가 오면 이들 동사보다 부정사가 미래의 시제를 뜻한다.

I *expect* you **to work** harder.
(=I expect that you will work harder.)

I *expected* you **to work** harder.
(=I expected that you would work harder.)

They **hope to be** amazing dancers.
(=They hope that they will be amazing dancers.)

② 완료부정사

❶ appear, seem, be said, be thought, be believed 등 뒤에 완료시제의 부정사가 오면 이들 동사 보다 부정사의 동작이나 상태가 먼저 일어난 것임을 뜻한다.

She *seems* **to have been** happy.
(=It seems that she has been(was) happy.)

She *seemed* **to have been** happy.
(=It seemed that she had been happy.)

You seem **to have made** a mistake yesterday.
(=It seems that you made a mistake yesterday.)

Rome is said not **to have been built** in a day.
(=It is said that Rome was not built in a day.)

I was disappointed **to have missed** the party.
(=I was disappointed that I had missed the party.)

❷ wished, wanted, hoped, expected 등 희망, 기대를 나타내는 동사의 과거형 뒤에 완료시제의 부정사가 오면 과거의 이루지 못한 행위를 뜻한다.

She *wished* **to have bought** the house.
(=She wished to buy the house, but she could not.)

(7) 독립부정사

To make matters worse, his five brothers all died, and he had to support their families.

Needless to say, this is not a good idea.

She can speak French fluently, **not to mention** English.

To tell the truth, it wasn't very good.

◈ 기타 독립부정사

to begin with, to be frank, to be brief, to say nothing of, not to speak of, not to say, so to speak, to be sure, strange to say, to make a long story short, to be honest, to sum up, to say the least (of it), etc.

EXERCISE

Ⅰ. Choose the correct form that would be acceptable in each sentence.

1. I had my mother (bring / brought) me an umbrella.
2. He helped me (find / finding) the post office.
3. The teacher made some students (cleaned / clean) the classroom again.
4. We shouldn't feel surprised (to learn / learning) that most young people have problems when they are growing up.
5. When the lemmings' food supply becomes too (low / lowly) to support the population, a singular migration commences.
6. Every time Cecily tried to get some advice from her father about withdrawing from college, he refused (discussing / to discuss) the matter.
7. Human nature is not a machine (to build / to be built) after a model.
8. Anesthetics are used (to cause / to causing) insensitivity to pain during surgical operations.
9. The policeman ordered the suspect (to not remove / not to remove) his hands from the hood of the car.
10. How well this plan will work remains (to be seen / to see).
11. She arranged to have the package (deliver / delivered) to the office overnight.
12. The manager will have a study (do / done) by the research department.

Ⅱ. Find an error in the underlined parts of each sentence and correct it.

1. The national train system helped a company creating a market nationally.

2. We cannot but being surprised to see how every creature is adapted to its surroundings.

3. As I walked along the hallway, I saw some people gathered around the elevator.

4. It is especially stupid for them to quarrel about which soccer team is the best.

5. We can cut down on the use of electricity to spend on lighting and air-conditioning.

6. An author may write a preface to describing how the book is organized and why it's organized that way.

7. Although Mark has been cooking for many years, he still doesn't know to prepare French foods in the traditional manner.

8. The purpose of inductive logic is to inferring general laws from particular occurrences.

9. Visitors were not permitted entering the park after dark because of the lack of security and lighting.

10. As time went on, he suffered such heavy losses that he was forced giving up his business.

11. People complain that the costs of establishing a business are so much that only the rich can afford running a company.

12. Darren let problems in his personal life to influence his performance at work.

Ⅲ. Choose the best completion for the following.

1. Stonehenge is said ____________ to predict the movement of the sun and moon.

   a. to be built　　b. to have been built

   c. to build　　d. to have built

2. Despite his broken leg, Tom can walk ____________ get around.

   a. good enough　　b. good to

   c. fine enough　　d. well enough to

3. To succeed in a difficult task, ____________.

   a. one needs to be persistent

   b. persistence is needed

   c. you need be a persistent person

   d. persistence is what one needs

4. To help a friend solve the problem troubling him, ____________.

   a. a man should be equipped with the kind of knowledge required

   b. nothing is better than the offering of one's money

   c. a friend should be made known of his difficult situation

   d. keeping one's promise is most important

5. It is very generous ____________ to do such a thing.

   a. you　　b. for you

   c. of you　　d. that you

6. The girls were sorry ____________ the singers when they arrived at the airport.

a. to had missed
b. to have missed
c. to be missed
d. to miss

7. We believe there ____________ an accident at the corner a short while ago.

a. is
b. to be
c. to have been
d. will be

8. The general manager will have his assistant ____________ the proceedings of the meeting and prepare a report for senior management.

a. to be transcribed
b. transcribed
c. transcribe
d. be transcribed

9. Your presence at the administrative office is required for the wage claim ____________.

a. to proceed
b. proceed
c. proceeding
d. proceeded

10. For further help ____________ the program, please refer to the instructions on our Web site or e-mail us with your specific question.

a. install
b. to install
c. installed
d. be installed

11. Several new waiters and salespeople were hired ____________ the influx of customers during the long holiday season.

a. handling
b. to be handling
c. to be handled
d. to handle

12. The candidate promised to ____________ prescription drug prices by as much as 30 percent if voted into office.

    a. low
    b. lower
    c. lowering
    d. having lowered

13. The training program offered by the company can help ____________ your future work options.

    a. broaden
    b. broad
    c. broader
    d. broadly

8 동명사(Gerund)

(1) 동명사의 역할

동명사는 명사의 기능을 가지며 주어, 목적어, 보어의 역할을 한다.

① 주어역할

Backpacking is a great way to travel.

Providing a loan will allow the bank to collect interest.

It makes a difference **reading** the instructions.

② 목적어 역할

She enjoys **playing** golf.

Regular exercise will help one avoid **being** overweight.

I get a lot of pleasure from **watching** my favorite TV shows.

The director aims at **reducing** corporate debt.

③ 보어역할

John's hobby is **listening** to music.

The key to happiness is **having** a lot of friends.

(2) 동명사의 시제

① 단순동명사: 동사원형+-ing

She is ashamed of **being** poor.
(=She is ashamed that she is poor.)

He insisted on my **finishing** the work.
(=He insisted that I should finish the work.)

② **완료동명사: having+p.p.**

He was blamed for **having abandoned** his team.
(=He was blamed that he had abandoned his team.)

I am sorry for you **having had** such a tedious time.
(=I am sorry that you had such a tedious time.)

③ **단순 수동형 동명사: being+p.p.**

He rejected **being sent** to a new department.
(=He rejected that he was sent to a new department.)

④ **완료 수동형 동명사: having been+p.p.**

She is proud of **having been educated** in the school.
(=She is proud that she was educated in the school.)

(3) 동명사의 의미상 주어

① 문장의 주어와 동명사의 의미상 주어가 같거나, 동명사의 의미상 주어가 일반인일 때 또는 동명사의 의미상 주어가 문맥상 분명할 때 동명사의 의미상 주어는 생략한다.

My daughter enjoys **playing** with her toy dog.

Driving a car requires patience and attention.

They blamed her for **doing** so.

② 문장의 주어와 동명사의 의미상 주어가 다른 경우 의미상 주어를 명시해야 한다. 동명사의 의미상 주어는 소유격으로 나타내는 것이 일반적이다. (* 구어체에서는 목적격을 쓸 때도 있다)

I'm surprised at **his(John's) making** that mistake.

This song is about **her realizing** that she is beautiful and deserves to live.

He insisted on **her paying** the money.

(4) 동명사를 목적어로 취하는 동사

miss, postpone, prevent, recall, recommend, resent, resist, risk, spend time, suggest, tolerate, understand, discuss, dread, enjoy, escape, excuse, finish, forgive, imagine, involve, mention, mind, admit, anticipate, appreciate, avoid, be worth, can't help, complete, consider, defer, delay, deny, detest, etc.

I don't **understand** your not **preparing for** the test.

We **appreciate your helping** us.

I **can't help getting** nervous.

We **discussed taking** a trip.

He **dreads taking** tests.

They **finished washing** the dishes.

She **spent** a lot of time **studying**.

(5) 전치사의 목적어로 동명사를 취하는 동사형

be afraid of	insist on
be excited about	plan on
be(get) tired of	succeed at(in)
be good(poor) at	think of(about)
be interested in	look forward to
be accustomed to	object to
be given to	plead innocent(guilt) to
be used to	

We are excited about going to the concert.

I'm thinking about getting season tickets.

I'm accustomed to spending a lot of time outdoors.

We're used to playing the guitar.

(6) 목적어로 동명사와 to부정사를 모두 갖는 동사

① 의미의 차이 없이 동명사와 to부정사를 모두 갖는 동사

begin, like, love, prefer, hate, start, intend, attempt, continue, cease, neglect, etc.

The bride started crying suddenly.

The bride started to cry suddenly.

② 의미의 차이를 가지고 동명사와 to부정사를 모두 갖는 동사

❶ remember, forget, regret : 동명사는 과거를, to부정사는 미래를 나타낸다.

I remembered to fill out the form. (미래의 일)

I remembered filling out the form. (과거의 일)

I forgot to turn off the light.

I forgot turning off the light.

❷ try : 동명사 '시도하다, 시험삼아 해 보다'
to부정사 '노력하다'

He tried steering the car on a slippery road.

He tried to steer the car on a slippery road.

❸ stop : 동명사 '~하는 것을 멈추다'
to부정사 '~하기 위해 멈춰서다'

When she came in, everyone stopped talking.

They stopped to see the rainbow.

③ [to+부정사] vs. [for+동명사]

I want a knife **to cut** the bread with now. (구체적인 목적어 수식)

A knife is a tool **for cutting** with. (일반적인 목적어 수식)

He hasn't got a chair **to sit on**.

A chair is a piece of furniture **for sitting on**.

(7) 수동의 의미를 가진 동명사

동사 deserve, need, require, want, be worth 등의 주어가 사물이고 목적어가 동명사일 때 수동의 의미를 가진다.

His conduct deserves praising. (=His conduct deserves to be praised.)

Your shoes need cleaning. (=Your shoes need to be cleaned.)

The problem needs solving. (=The problem needs to be solved.)

The problem needs to solve. (×)

⇒ 주어와 목적어의 관계가 수동이므로 to부정사의 능동형을 목적어로 쓸 수 없다.

> cf) The boy needs to wash.
> 주어와 목적어의 관계가 능동이므로 to부정사의 능동형을 목적어로 쓸 수 있다.

(8) 동명사의 관용적 표현

There is no accoun**ting** for tastes. (~할 수 없다)

It is no use your try**ing** to deceive me. (~해도 소용없다)

It goes without saying that health is more important than anything else. (~은 말할 필요도 없다)

I **cannot help** laugh**ing** at her. (~하지 않을 수 없다)

I **never** walk this lane **without** think**ing** of my highschool days. (~할 때마다 ~하다)

I **make a point of** tak**ing** exercise before breakfast. (~하는 것을 규칙으로 삼다)

He **came near** be**ing** run over by a bus. (~할 뻔하다)

I **feel like** hav**ing** beefsteak for supper. (~하고 싶다)

The garden **needs(wants)** weed**ing**. (~할 필요가 있다)

She **was on the point of** cry**ing** when he rang up. (막 ~하려고 하다)

He **is far from** tell**ing** a lie. (결코 ~하지 않다)

On graduat**ing** from school, I plan to apply for a job. (~하자마자)

In start**ing** a business, you should have enough confidence. (~할 때)

What do you say to go**ing** to the movie? (~하지 그래?)

Her suggestion **is worth considering**. (~할 가치가 있다)

My father **is busy** keep**ing** our store all day. (~하느라 바쁘다)

I am **look**ing **forward to** see**ing** you there. (~고대하다)

These are tomatoes **of my own** grow**ing**. (자신이 직접 ~한)

EXERCISE

Ⅰ. Choose the correct form that would be acceptable in each sentence.

1. Mary is used to (working / work) under deadlines and in high pressure situations.
2. Be careful to use appropriate (word / wording) when writing up the contract.
3. Studies have shown that a positive environment can significantly improve worker (effectiveness / effecting).
4. Many people cannot afford the cost of (obtain / obtaining) medical care without health insurance.
5. Her impressive volunteering record proves that Jessica is dedicated to (help / helping) others in need.
6. It would be wise of you to consider (renegotiating / to renegotiate) with your firm, as the job market is tough right now.
7. Do not forget (to sign / signing) the application form before submitting it to Mr. Kim at the front desk.
8. The chain was successful in (establishment / establishing) a new store.
9. A reversible chemical reaction is one that is capable (to go / of going) through a series of changes in either direction.
10. Civility is not a sign of weakness and sincerity is always subject to (prove / proof).
11. All good writing is swimming under water and (to hold / holding) your breath.
12. Women are used to (talk / talking) about their emotions and feelings.

13. The blog can't escape the danger of (revelation / revealing) private information.

14. Famous people get tired of (recognizing / being recognized) everywhere they go.

15. Mike is worried about (getting / being gotten) a bad grade.

16. (Learning / Being learned) a second language is easy for young learners.

17. She regrets (not to study / not studying) hard when she was younger.

18. Some universities strongly object to (admitting / being admitted) the disabled.

19. Robots aren't capable of (expressing / expression) their emotions.

20. It is no use (to persuade / persuading) him about the matter.

21. What we should keep in mind is (driving never / never driving) while drowsy.

22. He was ashamed of (having punished / having been punished) in front of his girl friend.

Ⅱ. Find an error in the underlined parts of each sentence and correct it.

1. It is generally believed that the government is responsible for protect its citizens from criminals.

2. A major issue at the Constitutional Convention of 1787 was the decision concerning the manner of election the President.

3. As a result of his inconsistency in represent his constituents, the senator was not reelected to the state legislature.

4. After to take the medication, the patient became drowsy and more

manageable.

5. We insist on you leaving the meeting before any further outbursts take place.

6. His father does not approve of him to go to the banquet without dressing formally.

7. Having lived here for seven years, my friend is used to speak English with all her classmates.

8. She is looking forward to go to Europe after she finishes her studies at the university.

9. Charlie assured his wife that there was no danger, but she could not help but worrying.

10. He narrowly escaped being ran over by a car.

11. I recall that I had a terrible struggle to find anything antireligious in the school libraries.

12. In addition to give money to health projects, he has given over $500 million to support education.

13. Most singers spend a lot of time in train to improve the quality of their voice.

14. Despite the persuasion, the witness denied seeing the accused.

15. Today's laws prevent a U.S. president from electing more than two times.

16. Preparing for a job interview, remember sitting up straight. This helps you look confident.

17. A good deal of time was devoted to understand the future requirements and how to begin incorporating these into our system.

18. Don't forget deleting the files in your computer when you finish the project.

19. The couple decided putting off inviting guests for their housewarming party.

20. We are very pleased hearing that you have been appointed regional manager for the Middle East.

21. They made such a firm decision that it was no good to try to persuade them.

22. Jimmy enjoys working as a regional manager, though the job makes him working like a bee.

23. Sally prefers finishing her daily tasks before going home to leave it undone.

III. Choose the best completion for the following.

1. ____________ your business card to individuals you meet will allow you to advertise your business in an inexpensive and effective way.
   a. Hands b. Handing c. Handed d. Hand

2. Age-related changes can contribute to one's having problems ____________ soundly.
   a. sleep b. sleeps c. slept d. sleeping

3. The promotion advisor, Mr. Dorsey, enjoys ____________ with potential clients during the open house days held once a month.

   a. talk b. talked c. talking d. to talk

4. By May, the weather should become warm enough to permit ____________ in the cellar or basement for longer periods of time.

   a. staying b. stay c. to stay d. stayed

5. Although they are satisfied with the training program, they object to ____________ to travel an hour each way to get to the training center and back.

   a. have b. has c. have been d. having

6. Despite ____________ more employees for the factory, the production manager still believes the facility is understaffed.

   a. having hired b. hired c. have hired d. were hired

7. The frozen dinner company is utilizing consumer ____________ on nutrition to formulate wholesome menus for its products.

   a. research b. to research c. researching d. researched

8. The bank has experienced a marked ____________ in deposits in recent weeks.

   a. increasing b. increase c. spending d. process

9. Upon hearing the bell ring, ____________.

   a. our departure was hasty.
   b. the students' departure was hasty.
   c. we departed hastily.
   d. the classroom was filled immediately.

10. Her plays are so difficult to understand that even the critics find difficulty ____________.

a. to explain them
b. and to explain them
c. to explaining them
d. explaining them

11. "What happens to your bag?" "It wants ____________."

a. to mend
b. mended
c. mending
d. mend

12. "I must remember ____________ John that the garden needs to be watered."

a. reminded
b. reminding
c. to be reminded of
d. to remind

13. The postman complained about ____________ by the dog.

a. attack
b. to be attacked
c. attacking
d. being attacked

14. As it is very cold outside. I'd rather ____________ at home tonight.

a. stay
b. staying
c. to stay
d. stayed

9 관사(Article)

(1) 부정관사 'a(an)'의 용법

① 단수 '하나'의 뜻으로 화폐, 시간, 거리, 무게 등 수를 동반한 단위와 함께 쓰인다.

a pound(￡1) a million pounds(￡1,000,000)

one and a half kilos(1½kilos)

a quarter(¼) a third(⅓) a fifth(⅕)

a half-holiday a half-portion a half-share

5p a kilo ￡1 a meter 10p a dozen

four times a day sixty kilometers an hour

② 어떤 일이 일어난 특별한 시간을 나타내기 위해 일, 월, 계절, 앞에 'one'으로 쓰인다.

One night there was a terrible storm.

One winter the snow fell early.

One day a telegram arrived.

One day(Some day) you'll be sorry you treated him so badly.

③ 사람 이름 앞에서 '~라고 하는 사람'의 뜻으로 사용된다.

A Mr. Johnson wants to speak to you.

④ 셀 수 없는 명사 앞에 놓여서 가산명사처럼 'a kind of'의 뜻으로 사용된다.

Asparagus is **a** grass.

⑤ 종족을 대표하여 '모든'의 뜻으로 쓰인다.

A tiger is a dangerous animal.

⑥ 작품, 제품을 뜻하기도 한다.

We can see **a** Rodin in his house.

⑦ 'a'가 생략되는 경우

❶ *turn*이나 *go*의 보어로 쓰인 명사 앞

He used to be a teacher till he **turned writer**.

❷ 직함이나 직책을 나타낼 때

Nelson became **Captain** of the Victory in 1800.

❸ rank, title을 한정하는 명사로 쓰일 때

He was promoted to the *rank* of **captain**.

He was given the *title* of **Earl**.

⑧ '같은, 동일한'의 뜻으로 쓰인다.

Two of **a** trade seldom agree.

⑨ 기타

How beautiful a day!

What a beautiful day!

Paul is **so good a student** that he is very popular in the class.

Nobody is **as diligent a man** as he.

He is **such a nice man** that everyone loves him.

Many a day has passed by without a line from him.

Jack is **quite a** gentleman.

She is **rather a** proud woman.

A spider(The spider) is an insect. (=Spiders are insects.)

I have never seen **a** UFO.

I'd like **a** coffee, please.

The United States is **a** democracy.

(2) 정관사 'the'의 용법

① 문맥에서 한 번 언급된 명사를 다시 지칭할 때

An intruder has stolen a vase; **the** intruder stole **the** vase from a locked cupboard.

② 화자와 청자가 대화 상황에서 분명히 알 수 있는 명사 앞

Open **the** window.

Please pass me **the** salt.

③ 수식어구에 의해 한정된 명사 앞

The house on the corner is for sale.

The boy who is standing by the door is my brother.

He explained **the** history of the building to us.

④ 유일한 대상 앞

The moon moves around **the** earth.

(the sky, the equator, the stars, the sea, the God, etc.)

⑤ 최상급, 서수, same, very 앞

The principal's office is on **the** second floor.

He is **the** same man that I saw on the bridge.

That's **the** very thing I was looking for.

The most effective way to lose weight is to stay on a balanced diet.

⑥ **the + 형용사/분사**: 사람을 나타낼 때는 복수보통명사로서 복수 취급하지만 일이나 상황 또는 예외적으로 특정 인물을 나타낼 때는 단수취급 한다.

The French like to eat well.

More schools for **the** physically **handicapped** need to be built.

The unexpected is bound to happen.

All **the accused** have pleaded guilty.

The accused was found innocent.

The deceased was a great scholar.

⑦ 신체 일부를 나타낼 때

❶ *catch, seize, take, hold, grasp, pull* + by the + 신체 일부

He caught me **by the hand**.

He held me **by the arm**.

She seized the child **by the collar**.

❷ *look, gaze, stare* + in the + 신체 일부

He stared me **in the face**.

❸ *strike, hit, touch, pat, punch, kiss, tap* + on the + 신체 일부

She hit him **on the ear**. (=his ear)

He punched me **on the chin**.

He patted me **on the shoulder**.

⑧ 단위 앞에서 each의 뜻으로 사용

We are paid by **the** hour. (시간당)

This cloth is sold by **the** yard. (야드당)

I am hired by **the** day. (일당)

Meat is usually sold by **the** pound. (파운드당)

⑨ the와 함께 쓰는 명사

산맥, 강, 운하, 대양	the Himalayas, the Alps, the Avon, the Pacific, the Thames, the Panama
방향, 계절, 자연현상	the north, the south, the left, the right, the rainy season, the East/West End
제도, 반도, 만	the West Indies, the Arabian Gulf, the Bahamas, The Korean Peninsula

악기 이름	the violin, the guitar, the piano
대학명 앞	the University of London
신문, 문학작품	the New York Times, the Observer
공공기관, 시설물: 호텔 극장, 클럽 박물관, 미술관	the Grand, the Hilton the Glode, the Athenaeum the British Museum, the National Gallery
특정 나라명	the Sudan, the Netherlands, the United States of America
배, 함대, 철도, 항공로	the Kyongbu Line
형용사를 가진 이름 앞	the late Mr. Smith, the young Mary

기타 'the'를 가진 표현	
the Smiths(Smith 부부, Smith 가족)	the Tower of London
the Middle East	the New Forest
the Bach Choir	the Philadelphia Orchestra
the Beatles	the Duke of York
the Sahara	the Yemen
the Gulf of Mexico	the Arabian Sea

⑩ 관사 없이 명사를 사용할 때와 관사와 함께 사용할 때

분류	관사 생략	관사 사용
계절	in winter in summer	After **the** winter is over, **the** swallows will return.
건물, 기관	be in bed leave town go to church	lie down on **the** bed approach **the** town admire **the** church
교통수단	by bicycle by bus by train by car	sit on **the** bicycle be on **the** bus take **the/a** train sleep in **the** car
식사	have breakfast before lunch stay for dinner	**the** breakfast was good he enjoyed **the** lunch **the** dinner was well cooked

질병	anaemia diabetes influenza	**the** plague (the) flu (the) measles (the) mumps
때, 시간	at dawn/daybreak at sunrise/sunset at dusk day and night evening came on before morning came	during **the** day admire **the** sunrise/sunset see nothing in **the** dusk in **the** daytime in **the** evening during **the** morning
고유명사	during Easter in England in Denmark Chicago	during **the** Easter of that year in **the** England of Queen Elizabeth in **the** Denmark of today **the** Chicago I like
대륙	North America Europe, Australia South Africa	**the** Antarctic **the** Arctic
도시	(downtown) Boston (ancient) Rome (suburban) London	**the** Hague **the** Bronx **the** city of London
기타	arm in arm day by day face to face from dawn to dusk from beginning to end from right to left from west to north	He took her by **the** arm. from **the** beginning of **the** day to the end of it keep to **the** right He lives in **the** north.

(3) 관사의 생략

신분, 관직, 호칭, 이름: **Dr.** Watson, **President** Pompidou, **Mr. and Mrs.** Johnson

Keep the change, **driver**.

I'm feeling a little better, **doctor**.

Waiter, bring me a glass of water, please.

과목: I like **history** very much.

English is more difficult than **mathematics**.

스포츠: He is a good player of **tennis**.

He plays **golf**.

가족관계: **Father** is generous, but **mother** is stingy.

축제일: Christmas Day, Independence Day, Passover(유월절)

달, 요일: January, February, March, April, … Sunday, Monday, Tuesday, …

나라명: Korea, Japan, Russia, Brazil, Scotland, …

호수, 산: Lake Windermere, Silver Lake, Mount Everest

추상명사 앞: Men fear death.
(**The** death of the Prime Minister left his party without a leader.)

(4) 주의해야 할 관용어구

out of question	= sure, undoubtful
out of the question	= impossible
behind time	= late
behind the times	= out of date, obsolete
of moment	= important, momentous
of the moment	= temporary, momentary
take place	= happen, occur
take the place	= act as a substitute

EXERCISE

I. Choose the correct form that would be acceptable in each sentence.

1. He explained (history / the history) of the building to us.
2. The Queen of (the Netherlands / Netherlands) visited Korea yesterday.
3. There is a cabin on (the island / island) where you want to stay.
4. They spent (most / the most) of their time playing computer games.
5. Do they sell butter by (a / the) pound?
6. The soccer ball hit me in (back / the back).
7. However (long a / a long) vacation, I always feel I want a few days more.
8. They had such (a fierce / fierce a) dog that no one could go near him.
9. Westbound travelers found (Rocky Mountains / the Rocky Mountains) the last great barrier before reaching the West coast.
10. The idea that the state should be neutral as to religion was perhaps thought "chilly" in (the 18th century / 18th century).
11. It has been announced that the Joint Chiefs of Staff will meet (the next week / next week)
12. We had to wait at (the airport / airport) for two hours because our plane was delayed.
13. He teaches (accounting / an accounting) in a private business school.
14. The most valuable metal was (the gold / gold).
15. Many of (the explorers / explorers) were financed by (monarchs / the monarchs) of different European kingdoms.

Ⅱ. Find an error in the underlined parts of each sentence and correct it.

1. Though the dust lay heavy upon the floor, it was evident that an old house, its windows carelessly boarded up, must once have been a magnificent mansion.

2. Prime Minister announced the names of those who were to be named to the Cabinet.

3. The trend towards attaching the designer's name to a whole range of products peaked in a summer of 1982 with a famous film star's salad dressing.

4. Although there are Spanish-speaking people in many parts of the United States, there is a particularly high concentration in South West.

5. The earth's climate remained same and unchanged for many millions of years during the jurassic peirod.

6. The benefit was such great a success that the promoters decided to repeat it.

7. The automobile industry is experimenting with a new type of a moter that will consume less gasoline and cause much less pollution.

8. Although the hail consists of ice or snow, it usually falls during the summer at the beginning of a thunderstorm.

9. Pension is a sum of money that is paid regularly by the government.

10. Europeans wanted metals so that they could make the coins for use in trading.

11. One of spices that Columbus found in the West Indies was allspice.

12. All of their early exploration were directed toward eastward routes.

13. The Arab merchants in the Middle East were also dealing in emeralds, rubies, and the silk.

14. Put it on scale so that I can see how much it weighs.

15. It usually takes 50 minutes to get downtown by the car from the airport.

Ⅲ. Choose the best completion for the following.

1. ______________ mathematics began in ancient Greece thousands of years ago.

   a. Study of the　　b. A study of the
   c. The study of　　d. Study of

2. ______________ more to be pitied than blamed.

   a. The uneducated are　　b. Uneducated is
   c. The uneducated is　　d. Uneducated are

3. The workers were paid ______________.

   a. by an hour　　b. by the hour
   c. by a hour　　d. in the hour

4. I like sports, of which ______________ is my favorite.

   a. a basketball　　b. the basketball
   c. basketball　　d. basketball game

5. Great Britain tried to persuade other nations to reduce their tariffs during ____________.

   a. nineteen century
   b. nineteen centuries
   c. nineteenth century
   d. the nineteenth century

6. We usually go out for ____________ because the hotel always serves the same.

   a. a lunch
   b. lunch
   c. the lunch
   d. the lunches

7. ____________ grew far away in India and Sumatra, and it was outrageously expensive.

   a. Pepper
   b. The pepper
   c. Peppers
   d. The peppers

8. ____________ who came from Spain are on board.

   a. All of passengers
   b. All of the passengers
   c. All of the passenger
   d. All the passenger

9. In ____________, the northern nations of Europe began to explore ____________ for a passage to China.

   a. the 16th century, Arctic
   b. the 16 century, Arctic
   c. the 16th century, the Arctic
   d. 16th century, the Arctic

10. It wasn't until ____________ that explorers were successful in reaching ____________.

   a. the late 1800s, the polar regions
   b. the late 1800s, polar regions
   c. late 1800s, the polar regions
   d. late 1800s, polar regions

10 분사(Participle)

(1) 현재분사, 과거분사

분사는 현재분사와 과거분사로 나뉘며 동사의 뜻을 가지고 형용사의 역할을 한다. 따라서 형용사와 마찬가지로 명사를 수식하거나 보어 역할을 한다.

	의미	예
현재분사(-ing)	진행, 능동(~하는, ~할)	I've never seen such a **boring** man.
과거분사(-ed, -en)	수동, 완료(~한, ~당한)	She was **surprised** at the news.

(2) 제한적 용법

분사형이 명사 앞 또는 뒤에서 명사를 수식한다.

There are leaves **fallen** on the ground.

The movie **directed** by Jack is about the end of the world.

This digital camera has some very **confusing** instructions.

The **stolen** money comes to more than 50,000 dollars.

He put some vegetables into the **boiling** water.

Can you understand the sentence **written** in Spanish?

(3) 서술적 용법

동사 뒤에서 주격보어 역할을, 목적어 뒤에서 목적격보어 역할을 한다.

① 주격보어

Sam looks a little **embarrassed** with the result.

It was **amazing** *to swim with hundreds of different types of fish.*

Some young people can feel **isolated** from their society.

② **목적격보어**

I hate shopping. I find *it* so **boring**.

He heard *a strange noise* **coming** from inside.

Brian had *his car* **stolen** while he was shopping.

(4) 현재분사와 동명사의 차이

	현재분사(능동, 동작의 진행)	동명사(의도, 목적)
명사수식	a **sleeping dog** (잠자는 강아지) a **rolling stone** (구르는 돌) **rising prices** (오르는 물가)	a **sleeping pill** (수면제) a **washing machine** (세탁기) a **smoking area** (흡연구역)
서술적 용법 (보어 역할)	He is **playing** computer games. (… 게임을 하고 있는 중이다)	My hobby is **collecting** insects. (… 곤충을 수집하는 것이다)

현재분사:

The woman **smiling** at me is my lovely wife.

People watched Thomas **smoking** in a public toilet.

I vividly remember the girl **selling** cookies in the cafeteria.

Some students are **taking** a nap in the middle of day after lunch.

동명사:

The **parking** lot officially has space for 200 cars.

She is trying on a wedding dress in the **fitting** room.

The employees kept **complaining** about welfare system of the company.

My sister is looking forward to **receiving** a big gift from Santa Claus.

(5) 감정을 나타내는 분사

주어가 감정을 느끼게 하면 현재분사를, 감정을 느끼는 주체이면 과거분사를 사용한다.

현재분사: His speech was very **boring**.

Playing computer games with him is **interesting**.

Her suggestion at the presentation was very **amazing**.

과거분사: I feel **relaxed** when I lie in a hot bath.

The result has made us **satisfied**.

We were **disappointed** with his speech.

현재분사 (주어가 감정을 유발시킬 때)	exciting, moving, shocking, boring, pleasing, amazing, interesting, satisfying, disappointing, dissatisfying, …
과거분사 (주어가 감정을 느낄 때)	excited, moved, shocked, bored, pleased, amazed, interested, satisfied, disappointed, dissatisfied, …

(6) 분사구문 형성 방법

ⓐ 부사절을 이끄는 접속사를 생략하고, 부사절의 주어와 주절의 주어가 같을 경우 부사절의 주어도 생략한다.

~~When you~~ go downstairs, you will find a tall woman.

~~As he~~ is loved by many students, he is very happy.

ⓑ 부사절의 시제와 주절의 시제가 같고 부사절 동사가 능동이면 '동사원형+ing'로, 수동이면 'being+p.p.'로 고친다. 이 때 'being'은 생략가능하다.

Going downstairs, you will find a tall woman.

(Being) loved by many students, he is very happy.

ⓒ 부사절의 주어와 주절의 주어가 다를 경우 부사절의 주어를 생략할 수 없다.

Although summer vacation came, I was not free from homework.
→ *Summer vacation* **coming**, I was not free from homework.

ⓓ 부사절의 시제가 주절의 시제 보다 한 시제 앞선다면 완료분사구문(having+ p.p.)으로 만든다.

As he had done it before, he knew how to do it.
→ **Having done** it before, he knew how to do it.

After the weather had improved, we enjoyed the rest of the game.
→ *The weather* **having improved**, we enjoyed the rest of the game.

When the sun had set, we started for home.
→ *The sun* **having set**, we started for home.

(7) 분사구문과 접속사절 전환

1. After he had repaired the car, the mechanic took it out for a road test.
   → **Having repaired** the car, the mechanic took it out for a road test.
2. As I didn't know the way, I had to ask for directions.
   → **Not knowing** the way, I had to ask for directions.
3. Being green with envy, Sarah bit her lip.
   → **As she was** green with envy, Sarah bit her lip.
4. If it is used economically, a tin will last for weeks.
   → **Used** economically, a tin will last for weeks.
5. When the signal was given, we set off.
   → **The signal being given**, we set off.
6. Having lost my purse, I could not buy the book.
   → **As I had** lost my purse, I could not buy the book.
7. As he had had nothing special to do, he just killed time.
   → **Having had** nothing special to do, he just killed time.
8. Exhausted after the match, he is studying for the final exam now.
   → **Though he was** (or has been) exhausted after the match, he is studying for the final exam now.
9. Because I was born in Korea, I am good at speaking Korean.
   → **Born** in Korea, I am good at speaking Korean.
10. Ann getting a nose job, nobody recognized her.
    → **Because Ann got** a nose job, nobody recognized her.
11. If you are allowed to do it, just go for it.
    → **Being allowed** to do it, just go for it.
12. After the team project was completed, the team members went for a ten-day vacation.
    → **The team project (being) completed**, the team members went for a ten-day vacation.

13. While Judy was waiting for a bus, a pickpocket approached her.
→ **Judy waiting** for a bus, a pickpocket approached her.

14. He got a call from someone and went out immediately.
→ He got a call from someone**, going out** immediately.

15. Benjamin works for a law firm and volunteers for the homeless.
→ Benjamin works for a law firm**, volunteering** for the homeless.

(8) 분사구문의 종류

① 시간: when, while, as soon as, before, after, as, until, etc.

While he was working as an official, he wrote his greatest novel.
→ Working as an official, he wrote his greatest novel.

② 원인, 이유: as, because, since

As she is loved by many friends, Mary is very happy.
→ (Being) loved by many friends, Mary is very happy.

③ 조건: if

If they are used properly, certain poisons prove beneficial.
→ Properly used, certain poisons prove beneficial.

④ 양보: although, though

Though all allowances are made for his inexperience, his salary is too small.
→ All allowances made for his inexperience, his salary is too small.

⑤ 연속동작: and

He took off his hat and smiled on me.
→ Taking off his hat, he smiled on me.

(9) 독립분사구문

부사절의 주어가 we, you, they, people 등 일반적인 주어인 경우 문장의 주어와 다르더라도 부사절 주어를 생략하고 분사구문으로 쓸 수 있다. 부사절의 주어와 주절의 주어가 다를 때 부사절의 주어를 생략하지 않는 경우도 독립분사구문에 포함된다.

Strictly speaking, getting into a major company is very difficult,

Judging from his accent, he must be a German.

Talking of fruit, I like melons best.

generally speaking, compared with, frankly speaking, considering (that), granted that, etc.

(10) 'with'를 가진 분사구문

He ran along **with his shirt hung**. (셔츠를 걸친 채)

He was standing **with his hands (being) in his pockets**. (주머니에 손을 넣은 채)

She fell asleep, **with the light turned on**. (불을 켜 놓은 채)

With night coming on, the orange light of sunset disappeared. (밤이 되면서)

EXERCISE

Ⅰ. Choose the correct form that would be acceptable in each sentence.

1. The Rosetta Stone is a large stone (covering / covered) in writing.
2. There is a long list of (endangering / endangered) animals.
3. The tourists still remain (isolating / isolated) in the mountains.
4. She sat (smiling / smiled) rightly on her father's knees.
5. Waves are caused by the wind (blown / blowing) over the surface of the sea.
6. We should have these shoes (polished / polishing).
7. Magma (moved / moving) inside a volcano causes lots of small earthquakes.
8. (Used / Using) an Internet service called the World Wide Web, you can access all kinds of information from computers all around the globe.
9. (Compared / Comparing) to Columbus' voyage, Magellan's expedition is a greater adventure.
10. The children were playing computer games, with the door (left / leave) open.
11. I was caught in the rain, with my body (shaken / shaking) with cold.
12. (Having spent / Spending) all the money last year, he started looking for a new job.
13. (Exhausted / Exhausting) after the match, he is studying for the final exam now.
14. With the new books (releasing / released), the staff members of the publisher had a party.

15. John stood there with his head (leaning / leaned) against the wall.

16. (Serving / Served) in the army, he learned a great deal about electricity.

17. He's a fountain of knowledge, (considering / considered) that he is still young.

18. (Seeing / Seen) under a microscope, a fresh snowflake has a delicate six-pointed shape.

19. (Angered / Having angered) by the decision, the lawyer quickly left the courtroom.

20. A deposit is required when (reserved / reserving) banquet space at his hotel.

21. Rain poured relentlessly, (dampened / dampening) the company picnic.

22. The (proposing / proposed) plan was acceptable to all members of the committee.

23. (Having heard / Heard) it all before, he didn't want me to repeat the whole story.

II. Find an error in the underlined parts of each sentence and correct it.

1. Parents shouldn't feel too surprising about these behaviors of teenagers; they are all parts of growing up.

2. There's a superstition among sailors that dolphins save drowned men by pushing them to the surface.

3. One way to use the energy of waves is to focus them into a narrow channel increased their power and size.

4. The new gene may improve crop quality, helped the plant to resist disease, insects, and extreme temperatures.

5. It was such shocked news that we couldn't believe it.

6. Not be able to understand English, she didn't know what you wanted.

7. Understanding the cultural habits of another nation is a complex bewildered task, but the rewards of knowing some of them are enormous.

8. The screaming burning victims were slowly lowered to the ground for medical attention.

9. Air law is defined as the body of law directly or indirectly is concerned with civil aviation.

10. Having eaten the cherry pie, I struck several pits and nearly broke a tooth.

11. The small shop recently won an award for the originality and outstanding quality of its handcraft pieces.

12. Due to a significant change in the nation's tax laws, we are likely to see to decrease investments by foreign individuals.

Ⅲ. Choose the best completion for the following.

1. ______________ the terrible weather forecast, we could not help it.

   a. Not having heard　　b. Not hearing

   c. As we did not hear　　d. Having heard

2. ______________, we had to walk home.

   a. The last train going　　b. The last train having gone

   c. Since the last train went　　d. The last train had gone

3. ______________, the two summits signed a peace treaty.

a. There were no objection
b. Being no objection
c. There being no objection
d. As there is no objection

4. ______________ round the world, Mark settled down in his native village.

a. Traveled
b. Being traveled
c. Having traveled
d. To travel

5. Chain reactions ______________ thermal or fast neutrons can be controlled in a reactor.

a. involve
b. involving
c. involved
d. are involved

6. Waves generally result from wind ______________ on water.

a. acts
b. acted
c. it acts
d. acting

7. Bifocal glasses are among the inventions ______________ Benjamin Franklin.

a. attributed to
b. have been attributed to
c. which attributed to
d. were attributed to

8. Frank told me that his offer of help was ______________.

a. to refuse completely
b. given to refuse
c. deteriorating to him
d. politely declined

9. The doctor, ______________, apologized.

a. his mistake realizing
b. he realized his mistake
c. realizing his mistake
d. realized his mistake

10. ______________ the law of the time, Margaret Sanger opened the country's first birth-control clinic in Brooklyn in 1916.

a. Disregarded
b. She disregarded
c. It was disregarded
d. Disregarding

11. Sheep are typically timid and defenseless, ___________ the leader and to flock together.

a. they are tending to follow　　b. tending to follow

c. with a tendency of following　　d. following the tendency of

12. Written in great haste, ___________.

a. Jim made a lot of mistake in the report

b. we found several mistakes in his letter

c. the book is full of errors

d. there are plenty of errors in the report

13. After taking this examination,___________.

a. he wanted to read the book

b. the book was read by him

c. the book made him happy to read it

d. the reading of the book gave him some pleasure

14. Having the highest marks in his class, ___________.

a. the college offered him a scholarship

b. he was offered a scholarship by the college

c. a scholarship was offered him by the college

d. a college scholarship was offered to him

15. Reading instruction, ___________, is a complete procedure.

a. it is properly conducted　　b. and proper conduction

c. properly conducting　　d. when conducted properly

16. ___________, Hong Kong acts as a gateway into and out of the Republic of China.

a. Strategically located　　b. Considering located strategically

c. It is located strategically　　d. Where strategically located

17. The resort keeps its patrons ____________ by offering numerous services that ensure their comfort and well-being.

a. satisfy b. satisfies c. satisfied d. satisfaction

18. Once ____________, both corporations will examine what alternatives are available for the affiliates they separately own.

a. merged b. merge c. are merged d. have merged

19. ____________ in the downtown area, the information center for expatriates provides various types of assistance and serves as a meeting place for young adults.

a. Locating b. Located

c. Having located d. Having been located

20. The hotel provides personal service and careful attention to detail, ____________ that you have a relaxing and comfortable stay.

a. be ensured b. ensure c. ensures d. ensuring

21. Readers find the young writer's first novel ____________ despite the fact that the initial reviews of the book were so dismal.

a. fascinate b. fascination c. fascinating d. fascinated

22. Dave was in Taiwan for three days ____________ as a tourist guide.

a. work b. be working c. worked d. working

23. We would like to know the departure date and the ____________ arrival date.

a. expect b. expecting c. expected d. expectation

11 전치사(Preposition)

(1) 전치사의 유형

① **단순전치사**: at, in, of, for, to, by, as, etc.

② **복합전치사**: along with, away from, out of, up to, due to, because of, by means of, in comparison with, in front of, etc.

(2) 전치사, 부사, 접속사의 비교

전치사	A car drove **past** the door.
	The dog was running **after** his master.
	All the students has a good time **but** John.
부사	A car drove **past**
	The dog was running **after**.
접속사	The dog came **after** I did.
	Most of the students had a good time **but** John did not. (=**but** not John)

(3) in, at, on

in	at	on
월, 년도, 계절, 때, 세기, 비교적 넓은 장소	시간, 시점, 비교적 좁은 장소	날짜, 요일, 특정한 날, 교통수단, 표면 위
in May, in July in 2019, in the evening in spring, in winter in the past, in the future in the 21st century in a town, in Seoul	at 10 o'clock, at 13:30 at noon, at midnight at this time tomorrow at the beginning of May at the bus stop at the station	on May 2nd, on Saturday on Thanksgiving day on my birthday on Sunday morning on Christmas night(day) on a bus, on a train

in a car, in the city in space, in the sky	at work, at home at the corner of the street	on the first floor on the ground
	기 타	
in the summer in 2002 in his youth in a moment, in a second in the end(결국) in time(때 맞추어) in a year(1년 후에) in three days(3일 후에) in five minutes(5분 후에) in the coming year (다음 해에) in place(제자리에) in the country	at the age of 19 at this moment at Christmas, at Easter at the end(~의 끝) at the end of the month at that time at the weekend at a party, at a meeting at a contest at times(때때로) at the latest(늦어도)	on the third day of July on the following day on 12 June 2019 on New Year's Day on time(정시에) on weekends on the street on the internet on TV on a regular basis (규칙적으로)

♣ Our office is **at** 62 East Avenue. (주소)

Our office is **in/on** East Avenue. (거리이름)

He lives in Geneva. (활동공간)

This train stops at Geneva. (지도상의 위치)

(4) for, during, through

for	during	through
정해진 시간, 기간동안 (주로 수 동반) for an hour for three years for the years for a long time	특정한 기간(시점)동안 during summer vacation during the exam during my stay during the spring	줄곧, 동안 내내 through a long sermon through the night through his life * throughout: 전반에 걸친, 도처에

(5) by, until(till), up to

① **by**: 특정 시기까지 동작의 완료

Contact the office to reschedule **by Sunday**.

By the time we'd walked five miles, we was exhausted.

We need to get home **by 8 o'clock**.

I should finish my homework **by tomorrow**.

② **until(till)**: 특정 시기까지 동작이나 상태의 계속

We didn't sleep **until midnight**.

We worked **until 6 o'clock**.

She didn't start eating **until food is served** to everybody.

Howard will stay here **till tomorrow**.

③ **up to**: 특정 시기까지 동작이나 상태의 계속 (~까지, ~에 이르기까지)

Up to last week, I hadn't received a reply.

He counted from one **up to thirty**.

He had lived in the house **up to the 19th century**.

This novel isn't **up to his best**.

> cf) **up to**: 의 마음대로인, ~의 책임인, ~에 달려있는
>
> It's **up to** you whether to go or not.
>
> The final choice is **up to** you.
>
> It's **up to** him to support his mother.

(6) since, from

① **since(~이래로)**: 과거부터 현재까지 계속되는 상황, 현재완료와 함께 쓰인다.

She has written several times **since** her departure.

We haven't seen our teacher **since** last week.

He has been working for this company **since** April.

② **from(~로부터)**: 시간의 시작점을 나타낸다.

From the moment he saw Jessica, he loved her.

From now on, I shall be stricter.

I started to walk **from** 8:00 in the morning.

(7) around, round, about[3]

① **around**: 주로 정지한 위치에 쓰인다.

We sat **around** the fire.

There is a store **around** the corner

They looked **around** the room.

You had better go out with a muffler **around** your neck.

② **round**: 주로 움직임을 뜻하나 정지된 위치에 쓰이기도 한다.

a tour **round(around)** the world, go **round** a corner

The ship had to go **round** the cape.

The earth moves **round** the sun (주변을 돌아서)

The members of the committee sat **round** the table. (주변에, 에워싸서)

③ **about**: 정지한 위치와 움직임 모두를 나타낸다.

There are trees dotted **about** the field. (들판 사방에)

We walked **about** the room impatiently. (방안을 이리저리)

He stood **about** the door. (문간 주위에)

3 '주위에'의 뜻으로 미국식 표현에서는 주로 around, 영국식 표현에서는 주로 round를 사용

cf) 부사 또는 다른 뜻의 전치사로 쓰일 때

I arrived **round** noon. (~무렵)

The tree is four feet **around**. (둘레)

around two hundred years ago (약)

turn **around** (방향을 돌리다)

all **around** (도처에)

He worked **round** the year. (1년 내내: 전치사)

He traveled Europe all year **round** (1년 내내: 부사)

He lives **round about** here. (주변에)

Tea was carried **round**. (골고루, 차례로)

Spring comes **round** soon. (순환하여)

(8) 기타 전치사를 가진 숙어 표현

at regular intervals 규칙적으로
at a good pace 상당한 속도로
at high speed 빠른 속도로, 급속하게
at a low price 낮은 가격으로
at 75 miles an hour 한 시간에 75마일로
on the recommendation of ~의 추천으로
under investigation 조사 중인
under development 개발 중인
by means of ~을 수단으로
for fear of ~을 두려워하여
with exception of ~을 제외하고
aside/apart from ~을 제외하고
out of print 절판된
out of room 공간이 부족한
out of season 제철이 아닌
out of reach 손에 닿지 않는
to my knowledge 내가 알기로는
along the side of ~의 측면을 따라
to one's satisfaction ~가 만족하도록
with no doubt 의심할 바 없이

at a charge of ~의 비용으로
at the rate of ~의 비율로
at one's expense ~의 비용으로
on the waiting list 대기자 명단에
under control 통제 하에
under pressure 압력을 받고 있는
under consideration 고려중인
under discussion 토론 중인
on account of ~의 이유로
with reference to ~에 관하여
with regard to ~에 관하여
without/but for ~이 없었다면
out of stock 제고가 떨어진
in addition to ~에 더해서
out of control 통제할 수 없는
to be sure 물론, 당연히
with no exception 예외 없이
without paying 무료로
beyond one's capacity 능력 밖인
with the aim of ~을 목적으로

with/in regard to ~에 관하여
with/in reference to ~에 관하여
concern over ~에 관한 걱정
equivalent/identical to ~와 동일한
as to/for ~에 관하여
against one's will ~의 의지에 반하여
comply with ~을 따르다
consist of ~로 구성되다
keep track of ~을 계속 알고 있다
depend/rely/count on ~에 의존하다
access to ~에 접근
permission from ~로부터의 허가
an advocate for(of) ~의 옹호자
a decrease/rise in ~에의 감소, 상승
in charge of ~을 책임지고 있는
in observance of ~을 준수하여
in violation of ~을 위반하여
regardless of ~에 상관없이
congratulate A on B A에게 B를 축하하다
difficulty in 동명사 ~에의 어려움
transfer A to B A를 B로 옮기다
have something to do with ~와 관련이 있다
entrust A with B A를 B에게 위탁하다
be proud of ~을 자랑스럽게 여기다
be ashamed of ~을 부끄럽게 여기다
take A for B A를 B로 여기다
deliver/save A from B A를 B로부터 구하다
remind A of B A에게서 B를 떠올리다
assure A of B A에게 B를 안심시키다
convince A of B A에게 B를 확신시키다
mistake A for B A를 B로 착각하다
exchange A for B A와 B를 교환하다
be anxious/eager for ~을 갈망하다
be famous/noted for ~으로 유명하다
be notorious for ~으로 악명높다
depend/count/rely/rest on ~에 의지하다
be acquainted with ~을 알다
thank A for B B에 대해 A에게 감사하다
punish A for B B 때문에 A를 벌주다

with respect to ~에 관하여
a dispute over ~에 대한 논쟁
an effect on ~에 대한 영향
respect for ~에 대한 존경
concerning/regarding ~에 관하여
account for ~을 설명하다
contribute to ~에 기여하다
comparable to ~에 필적하는
comparable with ~와 비교되는
absent from ~에 불참한
a cause/reason for ~의 원인/이유
exposure to ~에의 노출
a solution to ~에 대한 해결책
by means of ~의 수단으로
in honor of ~에게 경의를 표하여
in place of ~을 대신하여
on behalf of ~을 대신하여
as of 시간 ~로부터
direct A to B A를 B로 보내다
difficulty with 명사 ~에의 어려움
a problem with ~에 관한 문제
rob A of B A에게서 B를 빼앗다
ask for ~을 요구하다
be fond of ~을 좋아하다
be weary of ~에 싫증내다
be based on ~에 기반을 두다
be aware/conscious of ~을 알다
inform A of B A에게 B를 알리다
pass for ~으로 통하다
long for ~을 동경하다
search/look/seek for ~을 찾다
be grieved at ~에 슬퍼하다
be delighted at ~에 기뻐하다
be sorry for ~에 대해 유감이다
act on ~을 따라 행동하다
be sure of ~을 확신하다
be concerned with ~에 관여하다

blame A for B B에 대해 A를 비난하다
distinguish/know/tell A from B A와 B를 구별하다
deprive/rid A of B A에게서 B를 제거하다
cure/heal A of B A에게서 B를 치료하다
ease/relieve A of B A에게서 B를 덜어주다
supply/provide/furnish A with B A에게 B를 제공하다
prevent/keep/hinder A from B A가 B하는 것을 막다
be surprised/astonished/amazed/alarmed/startled at ~에 놀라다

EXERCISE

Ⅰ. Choose the correct form that would be acceptable in each sentence.

1. Last summer's heavy precipitation levels caused sales of beachwear to fall 20 percent (below / behind) normal.
2. The annex to the office building on Lester Avenue will be (under / in) construction until April.
3. The expansion project will be completed (by / until) December 20.
4. In observance (for / of) Labor Day, all US exchanges will be closed on Monday, September 6.
5. A recent report said consumer prices could exceed 4 percent (on / at) the end of the year.
6. A recent study mentions that prescription drug use has steadily increased (among / between) people aged 45 years and above over the past two decades.
7. Heavy rains have increased the water level behind dams (through / throughout) the country.
8. The country has suffered from little investment (until / over) the past year as a result of political instability.
9. All that construction will be completed (in / for) two months.
10. According to the weather forecast, the weather will be nice (at / on) the weekend.
11. I met Susan (at / on) the entrance to City Bank in the 5th street.
12. Mr. Johnson is going to Seoul (by / on) the plane that arrives before noon.

13. After the quality control process was changed, there has been a decrease (with / in) the number of defective products.

14. He is not very keen (on / with) drinking while discussing serious matters.

15. Older people usually have more difficulty (with / in) adapting themselves to new circumstances.

16. They are jealous (of / to) my high earnings and high popularity.

17. (For / During) several weeks, oil prices were frozen by presidential decree.

18. John had only one meal a day (for / during) the 4-week course.

19. He was never seen (from / since) that day on.

20. The amount of ozone decreased (for / during) the 1980s.

21. Thanksgiving celebrated on the fourth Thursday (on / in) November.

22. The repairman said that your car will be ready (until / by) lunch time on Monday.

23. If you go towards the canteen, you will see the toilets (in / on) the right.

Ⅱ. Find an error in the underlined parts of each sentence and correct it.

1. Employees expressed content with their salaries and working hours by the exception of those in packing, who requested a pay increase.

2. Except for rising oil prices, import prices went up by 16 percent in August.

3. Few companies have nursery facilities in spite of many of the employees are working mothers.

4. I phoned Mike and invited him to the party but he sounded like he didn't want to come.

5. I saw the advertisement for the company's annual sale of imported goods on today's newspaper.

6. If you want to be polite for them, you should reply to their letter by this week.

7. A lot of people were surprised by the explosion but no one knew who was responsible to the accident.

8. His secretary said that Mr. Kim had been out of the country since the last few days.

9. She reflected for a long time from what her friend had just told her.

10. It is interesting to compare the early stylized art forms of ancient to the modern abstract forms of today.

11. In his search to a building to purchase, he uncovered only two possibilities within the range he could afford.

12. The state of Washington, which entered the Union in 1889, was named for honor of George Washington.

13. When President Kennedy spoke in Berlin on behalf the American people, he was received with a show of enormous enthusiasm.

14. The army swept through the city as a pestilence.

15. Alike adults, young children find little difficulty in imitating sounds in foreign language.

16. While his lifetime, Frederick was awarded more than sixty patents for his inventions.

17. My hometown is about twenty miles by the east of Chicago.

18. The Rose Bowl parade takes place every year in Pasadena in New Year's Day.

19. I saw the advertisement at a newspaper yesterday and I want further information.

20. A lot of people called Paul and Mary and congratulated them about getting married.

21. At the intersection of 4th street and 8th avenue, you should turn left and you'll see the hotel in the end of the block.

Ⅲ. Choose the best completion for the following.

1. The rental deposit must be transferred to the landlord's bank account at least fifteen days ______________ the moving-in-date.
   a. by
   b. until
   c. due to
   d. prior to

2. Interest rates are falling ______________ a governmental push to raise all mortgage rates for middle class homeowners.
   a. according to
   b. even though
   c. in spite of
   d. in addition to

3. Companies can save hundreds on airfares ______________ computer linkups which allow for international meeting without leaving the office.
   a. above
   b. through
   c. into
   d. of

4. The manager said that _______________ any changes, the proposal would be presented at a special meeting of sustainable development organizations.

    a. barring   b. except   c. unless   d. because of

5. The company will not accept applications for transfers to overseas branches _______________ the first of the month.

    a. until   b. by   c. through   d. for

6. Wageworks Corporation is planning to lay off as many as 1,000 employees _______________ the next two years.

    a. at   b. by   c. until   d. over

7. We were on holiday for two weeks in Seattle, and _______________ those two weeks we didn't have a drop of rain.

    a. for   b. during   c. while   d. on

8. As a senior sales representative, his attitude _______________ buyers is full of confidence.

    a. for   b. with   c. toward   d. on

9. Singapore consists _______________ one main island and 63 other small islands.

    a. of   b. for   c. from   d. in

10. He compared the life in a small city _______________ the life in a big city.

    a. into   b. with   c. from   d. and

11. Most students were tired _______________ listening to their principal's speech.

    a. in   b. with   c. of   d. for

12. FC Barcelona has many good players capable ______________ detailed passing plays.

a. to　b. with　c. of　d. for

13. You should live with other people ______________ your lifetime.

a. for　b. during　c. for　d. in

14. We are going to give this special gift to them ______________ their wedding anniversary.

a. in　b. at　c. for　d. on

15. Matt has been working at a part-time job ______________ he graduated from high school.

a. from　b. until　c. by　d. since

16. I was surprised and ______________ a loss for what to do then.

a. at　b. on　c. in　d. for

17. If I can get ______________ with my exams, I'll take a long vacation.

a. under　b. beyond

c. behind　d. through

18. Jean ______________ a cold when she was in Los Angeles.

a. came by　b. came down with

c. came into　d. came off with

19. This fish is certainly ______________, but it is not the biggest in the shop.

a. above size in average　b. below average in size

c. over average in size　d. above average in size

20. Because he could not find the right theme ____________, his explanation was vague.

a. to center his thoughts around

b. around which his thoughts to center

c. on which to center his thoughts

d. in which to center his thoughts

21. ____________ rapid spread of railways and the increase in ocean transport, long-distance traveling became more common.

a. With the b. With c. When the d. Due to

22. Modern technological advances are being made, but ____________.

a. with highly considerable expense

b. at a great expense

c. with great expense involved

d. by a lot of expenses

23. The French are great bread eaters and the demand ____________ wheat has always been high.

a. for b. to c. with d. of

12 가정법(Mood)

(1) 가정법: 어떤 사실에 반대되거나 현실과 다른 가정, 상상, 희망 등을 나타낸다.

① **가정법 과거**: 현재 사실에 반대되는 상황을 가정

If+주어+동사의 과거형(또는 were)~, 주어+조동사의 과거형+동사원형… [만일 ~라면, …할 텐데]

If I **were** you, I **would not go** there alone.

If she **had** time, she **might go** to the party.

If all people **valued** human life, there **would be** no crime.

If you **didn't pass** the red light, you **wouldn't face** 50-dollar fine.

If she **were** not thankful for small blessings, she **couldn't be** happy herself.
(= As she is thankful for small blessings, she feels happy herself.)

② **가정법 과거완료**: 과거 사실에 반대되는 상황을 가정

If+주어+had p.p.~, 주어+조동사의 과거형+have p.p.… [만일 ~했다면, …했을 텐데]

If I **had known** the fact, I **would have told** it to you.

If I **hadn't driven** so fast, I **wouldn't have had** an accident.

If I **had been born** in America, I **could have spoken** English fluently.

If she **had studied** hard enough, she **would have passed** the test.

If you **hadn't made** a mistake, you **could have passed** the exam.
(= Because you made a mistake, you couldn't pass the exam.)

If I **hadn't stayed** up all night, I **wouldn't have been** very tired.
(=Since I stayed up all night, I was very tired.)

③ **가정법 미래:** 미래에 대한 의심이나 불가능한 사실을 가정

If+주어+were to 동사원형~, 주어+조동사(현재/과거)+동사원형… should [만일 미래에 ~한다면, …할 텐데]

If someone **were to** give you a million dollars, what **would** you do?

What **should** I do if by any chance I **should** fail?

If you **should** see Harry, **give** him my regards.

If I **were to** be young again, I **would** work harder.

★ If 조건절의 현재형이 미래시제를 대신할 수 있으므로 실제로 가정법 미래형을 따로 구분하여 사용하지 않는 경우가 많다.

가정법 현재형은 현재 또는 미래에 관한 의심이나 불확실성을 나타내며 단순조건절로 취급하기도 한다.

If+주어+동사원형/동사의 현재형~, 주어+조동사의 현재형+동사원형… [만약 ~한다면, …할 텐데]

If it **rain** tomorrow, I **will** not go.

If you **come** this weekend, we **can** have more time to talk.

(2) 혼합가정법

if-절과 주절의 내용상 시점이 다른 경우 혼합가정법을 사용한다.

① **if-절:** 가정법 과거완료　　**주절:** 가정법 과거

If+주어+had p.p.~, 주어+조동사의 과거형+동사원형…

If I **had taken** your advice then, I **should** be happier now.
(과거에 당신의 충고를 받아들였다면 지금 내가 더 행복할 텐데)

If she **had not died**, she **would** be sixty this year.
(그녀가 세상을 떠나지 않았다면 올해 60세가 될 텐데)

② **if-절**: 가정법 과거 **주절**: 가정법 과거완료

If+주어+동사의 과거형~, 주어+조동사의 과거형+have p.p.…

If he **were** a man of strong will, he **would have succeeded**.
(그가 강한 의지를 가진 남자라면 과거에 성공했었을 텐데)

(3) as if(as though) 가정법

① 직설법 현재 + as if 가정법 과거

She sings beautifully as if she were a professional singer.
(= In fact, she is not a professional singer but she sings beautifully.)

They talk as if they knew the truth about the accident.
(= In fact, they don't know the truth about the accident.)

② 직설법 현재 + as if 가정법 과거완료

She sings beautifully as if she had been a professional singer.
(= In fact, she was not a professional singer but she sings beautifully.)

Donald talked as if he had seen the movie.
(= In fact, Donald didn't see the movie.)

She talked as if she had been a graduate of New York University.
(= In fact, she wasn't a graduate of New York University.)

(4) wish 가정법

① I wish 가정법 과거

I wish I were tall enough to water the plants on the top shelf.
(= I'm sorry I'm not tall enough to water the plants on the top shelf.)

I wish my son won a gold medal at Olympic Games.
(= I'm sorry my son doesn't win a gold medal at Olympic Games.)

② **I wish 가정법 과거완료**

I wish I hadn't set out to search the haunted house.
(= I'm sorry I set out to search the haunted house.)

I wish they had finished their homework earlier.
(= I'm sorry they didn't finish their homework earlier.)

(5) without 가정법

① **without 가정법 과거:** [~가 없다면, ~일 텐데]

Without science, our lives **would** be very inconvenient.
(= **But for** science, our lives **would** be very inconvenient.)
(= **If it were not for** science, our lives **would** be very inconvenient.)
(= **Were it not for** science, our lives **would** be very inconvenient.)

② **without 가정법 과거완료:** [~가 없었다면, ~이었을 텐데]

Without a great director, this movie **could never have been** made.
(= **But for** a great director, this movie **could never have been** made.)
(= **If it had not been for** a great director, this movie **could never have been** made.)
(= **Had it not been for** a great director, this movie **could never have been** made.)

(6) It is time＋가정법 과거/should＋동사원형

(가정법 현재를 동반하기도 하며 보통 that을 생략함)

It is (high) time you **began** to improve your ability.

It's time we **do** something.

It's time you **washed** your shirt. (= It's time you should wash your shirt.)

(7) 가정법과 직설법 문장

If he hadn't been incompetent, he might not have been fired from his company.
(= Since he was incompetent, he was fired from his company.)

If the building sign had been written in Korean, they couldn't have read it.
(=As the building sign wasn't written in Korean, they could read it.)

If it hadn't rained yesterday, the road wouldn't be muddy today.
(= In fact, it rained yesterday, and the road is muddy today.)

If he hadn't posted bad message on the Internet, he wouldn't be in trouble.
(= In fact, he posted bad message on the Internet, he is in trouble.)

Thomas acts as if he had been very close to Jenifer.
(= In fact, he wasn't very close to Jenifer.)

He acts as if he didn't cut the cheese at table.
(= In fact, he cuts the cheese at table.)

I wish that she could smile at me.
(= I'm sorry that she can't smile at me.)

Were it not for smart phones, we would not waste much time.
(= As we have smart phones, we waste much time.)

Without my alarm clock, we would have been late for school.
(= In fact, I had an alarm clock, and we didn't late for school.)

(8) 기타표현

① If-절을 생략하고 가정법을 나타내는 경우

You **could have done** no better.
(더 잘할 수 없었을 것이다/실제로 최선을 다했다)

I **would not have taken** the doctor's degree.
(박사학위를 받지 못했을 것이다/실제로 박사학위를 받았다)

He **might have listened** to our complaints.
(우리 고민을 들어주었을 것이다/실제로 들어주지 않았다)

They **should have limited** the use of automobiles.
(자동차의 사용을 제한했어야 했다/실제로 제한하지 않았다)

② **If 대용 접속사로 가정법을 나타내는 경우**

Provided you were in his place, what would you do?

You can use my car **on condition that** you bring it back tomorrow.

I prefer to go by bus, **providing that** the traffic is not heavy.

That is not a problem **as long as** you keep the deadline.

Suppose (that), Unless, Providing (that), Granted/Granting (that), on condition (that), in case (that), so long as

③ 부사어구 형태의 조건절

I drove at full speed, **otherwise**, I might have missed the last train for Seoul.
(= I drove at full speed, **if I had not driven at full speed**, I might have missed the last train for Seoul)

With your assistance, I should certainly succeed.
(= **If you would assist me**, I should certainly succeed.)

What would you do **in my place**?
(= What would you do **if you were in my place**?)

④ 부정사, 분사구문 형태의 조건절

To see her dance, you would burst out laughing.
(= **If you saw her dance**, you would burst out laughing.)

We should be happy **to accompany you**.
(= We should be happy **if we could accompany you.**)

Stripped, he must have been a fine figure of a man.
(= **If he had been stripped**, he must have been a fine figure of a man.)

Going upstairs, you'll see a big red door.
(= **If you go upstairs**, you'll see a big red door.)

⑤ 주어로서의 명사 조건절

A true friend would not leave you in need.
(= **If he were a true friend**, he would not leave you in need.)

A man who has common sense would not do it.
(= **If he had common sense**, he would not do it.)

An ordinary man would not know where Easter Island is.
(= **If he was an ordinary man**, he would not know where Easter Island is.)

EXERCISE

I. Choose the correct form that would be acceptable in each sentence.

1. If I were employed, I (could / can) afford a bigger house.
2. If ocean water weren't salty, it (wouldn't be / wouldn't have been) dangerous for us to drink.
3. If you (speak / spoke) less and (listen / listened) more, you will be much more popular.
4. She didn't study hard enough, so she didn't pass the test.

   = If she (had studied / studied) hard enough, she (would pass / would have passed) the test.
5. If I (realized / had realized) the baby was sleeping, I wouldn't have made so much noise.
6. I need some help with my homework. I wish Tom (is / were) here now to help me.
7. I failed the exam because I did not study. I wish I (studied / had studied).
8. You're the best teacher I've ever had. I wish you (would be / had been) my teacher last year as well.
9. Mary was caught while cheating on the exam. But she behaved as if nothing (happened / had happened).
10. If the quality of the product (is / were) not good enough, they will not buy it.
11. (Should / Would) I be allowed to do so, I will ask for permission to go there.
12. It's about time that you (ask / asked) the manager for a pay rise.

13. I'd give up my present job (provided / unless) I liked it very much.

14. Provided you (lose / will lose) the checks, you'll need to phone this number.

15. A porter will come if you (ring / will ring) the bell.

16. That city has terrible smog; otherwise, I (can / could) enjoy living there.

17. The educational system is not adequate, and they cannot train many doctors.

    = If the educational system (is / were) better, they (could / can) train many doctors.

18. We (should have sold / would have sold) our house before the company built the factory across the road. ('regret for not selling our house at that time')

19. (Should / Could) your rental application be denied, the owner of the apartment will refund the cost of processing the application.

20. But for the dedicated efforts of our staff, the business (will / would) have crumbled under the competition.

Ⅱ. Find an error in the underlined parts of each sentence and correct it.

1. If I were in your situation, I will tell him not to force customers to buy products they don't need.

2. I wish I weren't busy yesterday, and I could have helped you to finish the work.

3. A: Do you know if she had any problems these days?

   B: It appears as if she lost interest in her job.

4. Jimmy, who has been working as an auditor for more than 10 years, looks though he didn't have anything to do with accounts.

5. They wish that the company doesn't have to much money invested in those items which were selling slowly.

6. A warranty tells about the quality of a product and about what the company will do if something were wrong.

7. If you paid the invoice within 10 days after you had received it, you could have taken a 3 percent discount.

8. Supposed Sally hadn't checked the figures, could we have found the mistakes?

9. I would rather you do what you thought was right.

10. We will give them a longer lunch-break as long as they will agree to start earlier.

11. Had you told me you were free this evening, I had cancelled the appointment.

12. I wish fewer people drove cars. If fewer people drove cars, the air will be cleaner.

13. The company should never have won the account without the support of the very talented copywriters in the advertising division.

14. If insolvency laws do not change and continue to favor creditors, many small-scale companies goes bankrupt.

15. It is most important that he speaks to the dean before leaving for his vacation.

16. If it were possible for us to bring back the past at will, how happy we shall be.

17. If a crisis would occur, those unfamiliar with the procedures would not know how to handle the situation.

18. During the meeting, nearly all of the members demanded that the rules were suspended so that a report could be given.

19. If England had won the Revolutionary War, the whole history of the English-speaking world would be different.

20. Were to you arrive before the office is open, the security guard will let you in.

21. She wishes that we didn't send her the candy yesterday because she's on a diet.

22. The political candidate talked as if she has already been elected to the presidency.

23. I wish we had chosen a slight less expensive hotel to stay at.

Ⅲ. Choose the best completion for the following.

1. Mr. Watson wishes that everyone ______________ not say anything about this meeting to anyone.

   a. could　　b. would

   c. had　　d. was

2. If customers order a large number of items at a time, vendors ____________ discounts to the customer.

a. give
b. would give
c. would have given
d. gave

3. They requested that we ____________ read the instructions carefully.

a. will
b. might
c. should
d. had

4. So lone as two or more things ____________ the same in quality, customers usually buy the one with the lowest price.

a. will be
b. were
c. had been
d. are

5. It is essential that any caller ____________ immediately whether he is speaking to the office he requires.

a. will know
b. should know
c. have known
d. knew

6. If they had planned this properly, they ____________ in this mess now.

a. may not be
b. would not be
c. have been
d. will not be

7. ____________ a world war to start, it would be the most terrible.

a. Were
b. Was
c. Should
d. Would

8. James Watt invented the steam engine in the 1700s; otherwise, the Industrial Revolution ____________ begun then.

a. should not have
b. must not have
c. might not have
d. could not have

9. People could not have grown crops in many areas if they ____________ how to irrigate.

a. hadn't learned
b. had learned
c. didn't learn
d. learned

10. Had Einstein not lived, we ____________ a much different world today.

a. might have had
b. would have had
c. will have
d. would have

11. The recurring problem of unheated rooms would ____________ if the owner had responded to the tenants' initial complaints.

a. have elimination
b. have been eliminated
c. had been eliminated
d. have been eliminating

12. If plans ____________ made sooner, they would be conducting the feasibility study for the Safeway Water Project by now.

a. were being
b. was being
c. had been
d. have been

13. ____________ the machine parts arrived promptly, we would have been able to finish assembling the machine in time for its first run.

a. Had
b. Should
c. Were
d. Have

14. If preparations ____________ for the presentation, it would have been much easier to sell the proposal.

a. had been made
b. had made
c. were made
d. would be made

15. _____________, he would have been able to pass the exam.

a. If he studied more

b. If he were studying to a greater degree

c. Had he studied more

d. Should he study more

16. Ben would certainly have attended the meeting _____________.

a. if he didn't get a flat tire

b. if he had not had a flat tire

c. Had he had a flat tire

d. Had the tire not flattened itself.

17. A more skillful teacher _____________ such a child otherwise.

a. have been treated

b. would have treated

c. have treated

d. would have been treated

18. If he _____________ in Vietnam war, he would be 39 years old now.

a. has not been killed

b. wouldn't be killed

c. had not been killed

d. weren't killed

19. If you had been hit that time, we _____________ you now.

a. would not have seen

b. have not seen

c. would not see

d. should not have seen

20. If only they _____________ their house ten minutes earlier, they would have arrived at the opera in good time.

a. had left

b. left

c. have left

d. should left

13 접속사(Conjunction)

(1) 등위접속사: 단어와 단어, 구와 구, 절과 절을 대등한 관계로 연결하는 접속사

and, but, or, so, nor, either A or B, both A and B, neither A nor B, etc.

Which do you like better, tea **or** coffee?

He heard the explosion **and** phoned the police.

Robert is secretive **but** David is candid.

He didn't want their help, **but** he had to accept it.

You can sleep on the couch, (**or**) go to a hotel, **or** go back to your home.

It was raining, **so** I put on my rain coat.

They disliked John, **and** that's not surprising. (그런데)

Give me some money, **or** I'll take it. (그렇지 않으면)

Tell me about the fact, **and** I'll help you escape. (그러면)

He was unhappy about it, **and yet** he did what he was told. (그러나)

(2) 등위상관접속사: 2개의 술부, 목적어, 동사, 부사를 연결하는 접속사

either A or B, neither A nor B, both A and B, as ~ as, so ~ as, such ~ that, no sooner ~ than, whether ~ or, the 비교급~ the 비교급, etc.

You can make your payment **either** in person **or** by mail.

It depends on **neither** who you are **nor** what you know.

There will be a party tonight, **for** he is retiring this week.

Both coffee **and** tea have long and historic pasts.

He didn't come to help but to hinder us.

Not only did they break into his office and steal his books, **but** they **also** tore up his manuscripts.

> cf) - He did **not** want to ask them for help; (but) **nor** could he do without their help.
> - We owe **no** money, and **neither** do they.

(3) 부사절을 이끄는 종속접속사

시간	when, while, as, as soon as, since, until, before, after, once
이유	because, as, since, now that, in that
목적	so that, in order that, lest ~ should
결과	so/such ~ that ~
조건	if, unless, given (that), in case (that), provided (that), supposing (that), seeing that, considering (that), as long as …
양보	though, even though/if, no matter+의문사

As soon as he saw me, he started to run away.
= **On seeing** me, he started to run away.
= **No sooner** had he seen me **than** he started to run away.
= **The moment** he saw me, he started to run away.
= **Hardly** had he seen me **when(before)** he started to run away.
= **Scarcely** had he seen me **before(when)** he started to run away.

Now that the tennis court is dry, let's play tennis.

Be careful **lest** you **should** fall on the ice.

He studied **so** much **that** he was always at the top of his class.

Sophia did yoga every day **so that** she could maintain a slim figure.

A smart phone is **so** useful **that** most people use it these days.

He had **such** a good voice **that** we could understand every word he said.

(4) 접속부사

however, in contrast, on the contrary, on the other hand, therefore, hence, thus, as a result, consequently, finally, in short, all in all, besides, moreover, in addition, in other words, that is to say, by the way, for instance, etc.

Once Jack decides to do something, nobody can change his mind.

Unless you eat plenty of fruits, you may need to take a supplement of Vitamin C.

Since it is possible to breathe fresh air, some people want to live in the countryside.

I didn't make any mistake. **As a result**, I passed the exam.

The dinner was delicious. **Nevertheless**, we felt that it was overpriced.

Whereas she fills out the tax forms, he does the shopping and most of the cooking.

EXERCISE

Ⅰ. Choose the correct form that would be acceptable in each sentence.

1. Kate didn't get the job (although / as though) she had all the necessary qualification.
2. (Although / Since) Rhode Island is much smaller than Texas, it has the same number of senators.
3. The storm was (so severe that / such severe that) all electrical power in the state was knocked out for a week.
4. (Like / As) the committee has written in its current report, the rules need to be enforced more strictly.
5. Baby girls are not fed as much as their brother, (nor do the girls / nor the girls) get as much attention.
6. Patty hasn't read the chapter, (nor has she / nor she has) written her essay.
7. Not only (is her boss / her boss is) dishonest, but also he is temperamental.
8. Jassem will return to his country, (since / for) he is tired of living away from home.
9. Neither Jassem nor Julie still (live / lives) in Santa Barbara.
10. Women are still slower than men in some long-distance swimming events. (Nevertheless / Moreover), they are swimming faster today than many of the men's champions of the past.
11. All new computer technicians should receive (adequate / adequacy) and up-to-date training in the use and maintenance of state-of-the-art equipment.

12. To create a (last / lasting) effect on the public, the firm utilizes hidden advertising in all of its print and television ads.

13. Candidates will be considered on the basis of their prior experience (as well as / in addition) on their level of dedication and loyalty.

14. Societies have been developing (since / as) the first humans walked on the Earth.

15. When she wakes up, her father (will already have left / will already leave) for work.

16. I'm going to bathe my baby just as soon as she (will finish / finishes) eating.

17. A child's brain is one mass, (while / however) an adult's brain is separated into two hemispheres.

18. The gorilla, as well as the chimpanzee and the orangutan, (walks / walk) on its hind legs.

19. Many birds have developed extraordinary eyesight. (Similarly / As a result), the eyesight of humans has improved greatly through the ages.

20. The Y chromosome weakens males; (otherwise / likewise), men would live as long as women.

Ⅱ. Find an error in the underlined parts of each sentence and correct it.

1. Even though the men were the leaders in the society; nevertheless, within the family, they were subordinate to the women.

2. In Madagascar, the women are such aggressive buyers and sellers so that they dominate the marketplace.

3. George said he would contact me but he didn't phone also write to me.

4. The restaurant was such crowded that we couldn't find anywhere to sit down.

5. Few companies have nursery facilities in spite of many of the employee are working mothers.

6. Cayenne pepper comes from the seedpod of the pepper plant, which is dried or then powdered.

7. The element ruthenium is hard and brittle, and does not dissolve in either water nor acid.

8. Though both cats and dogs existed before man, without man neither one group and the other would have developed so many varieties.

9. The reason he has been such a success is because he never gives up.

10. A catalytic agent such as platinum may be used so the chemical reaction may advance more rapidly.

11. Either John had to pay the phone bill or lose his phone.

12. If you placed an order, then have not received your package, please wait two months from the day it was shipped before making an inquiry.

13. Joe goes to Paris next week, but when I saw him, he hasn't bought his ticket yet.

14. Because her tireless work with the impoverished and the sick, Mother Teresa was awarded the Nobel Peace Prize in 1979.

Ⅲ. Choose the best completion for the following.

1. The child appears healthy; ____________, it's good idea for her to have a checkup soon.

   a. otherwise　　b. therefore　　c. nevertheless　　d. moreover

2. To lead a peaceful life, women should not try to do too much, nor ____________ do too little

   a. should they　　b. they
   c. they should　　d. they shouldn't

3. We need to send the letter first class ____________ it'll get there by the end of this week.

   a. after　　b. as soon as
   c. so that　　d. while

4. These negotiations are in the early stages, ____________ we are confident that a contract will be signed.

   a. and　　b. but　　c. so that　　d. or

5. You'd better write your name and address on your bag ____________ you lose it.

   a. as far as　　b. while　　c. in case　　d. so that

6. Traveling by car will be more convenient ____________ we can find somewhere to park.

   a. while　　b. although　　c. in case　　d. as long as

7. He decided to stay in the office for a few hours that evening and ____________ in early the next morning.

   a. came　　b. come　　c. coming　　d. became

8. Changes come slowly and almost imperceptibly, ____________ they do come.

a. but　　b. so that　　c. or　　d. and then

9. Jean had not realized how long the magazine was or ____________.

a. its reading difficulty

b. that it was so difficult to read

c. how difficult it was to read

d. its difficulty in reading

10. Paul delayed his departure until morning, ____________.

a. being tired and afraid about driving at night

b. for fear of driving at night and tiredness

c. being fearful to drive at night and being tired

d. for he was tired and afraid to drive at night

11. Not all technology is based on science, ____________ is science necessary to all technology.

a. it　　b. nor　　c. and　　d. but

12. Mr. Roberts is a noted chemist ____________.

a. and a very efficient teacher too

b. as well as an effective teacher

c. but he teaches very good in addition

d. however he also teaches very good

13. ____________ of a newspaper nor the number of pages in an edition has ever been standardized.

a. Neither the page size　　b. Neither is the page size

c. The page size is neither　　d. The page size, neither

14. Researchers have recently confirmed ____________ Pygmies are missing an insulin like growth factor.

a. and that b. because c. so that d. that

15. Scientists have concluded ____________ rainfall and general weather conditions.

a. what affects sunspots that b. what affects sunspots
c. that sunspots affect d. that what sunspots affect

16. The question is whether people will continue to compound the problems of the environment ____________.

a. or will adjust to and improve it b. and adjust to or improve it
c. or adjust to by improving it d. or adjusting and improving it

17. Jane can't stand it ____________ noises during a concert.

a. when people make b. if the music is disturbed by people's
c. if people have d. when people do

18. If photosynthesis ____________ stop, most living things would disappear from the Earth in a few years.

a. will b. were to c. were d. would

19. The theater manager told you not to let anyone in ____________ you his ticket.

a. without him to show b. unless him showing
c. unless he shows d. without he should show

20. All examinees should bring ____________ a driver's license or passport and a pencil to the testing center.

a. or b. and c. either d. both

참고문헌

능률영어교육연구소(2017).「문제로 마스터하는 고등영문법」. NE능률.

이동기(2016).「(한 권으로 정리하는) 핵심문법 500제」. 법문사.

이재옥(1999).「이재옥 BASIC TOEFL」. 소명.

이종한(2017).「쉽게 풀어쓴 고급 영문법」. 밥북.

전수인(2007).「실전영문법의 완성」. 민사고.

해커스 어학연구소(2017).「해커스토익 실전 1000제 3 READING」. 해커스 어학연구소.

BOB WALSH(1999).「TOEIC 실전영문법」. 혜지원.

David Cho(2008).「해커스토익 READING」. 해커스 어학연구소.

David Cho(2015).「Hackers TOEFL READING」. 해커스 어학연구소.

Altenberg, Evelyn and R. M. Vago(2010). *English grammar: Understanding the basics*. Cambridge: Cambridge University Press.

Azar, Betty S. and S. A. Hagen(2016). *Understanding Using English Grammar*(5th ed.). NY: Pearson Education.

Berry, Roger(2011). *English grammar: A resource book for students*. NY: Routledge.

Ehrlich, Eugene(2011). *English grammar*(3rd ed.). NY: McGraw-Hill.

Goldstein, Barbara(2013). *Grammar to go*(4th ed.). Boston: Cengage Learning.

Murphy, Raymond(2012). *English grammar in use: a self-study reference and practice book for intermediate learners of English: with answers*(4th ed.). NY: Cambridge University Press.

Murphy, Raymond(2009). *Grammar in use intermediate with answers self-study reference and practice for students of English*[v. 1 Student's book]. Cambridge: Cambridge University Press.

Rothstein, Evelyn(2009). *English grammar instruction that works!: developing language skills for all learners*. Thousand Oaks, Calif: Corwin Press.

Smalzer, William(2009). *Grammar in use intermediate workbook with answers*(3rd ed.). NY: Cambridge University Press.

Swan, Michael(1995). Practical English Usage(2nd ed.). Oxford: Oxford University Press.

Thomson, A. J. and A. V. Martainet(1986). *A Practical English Grammar*(4th ed.). Oxford: Oxford University Press.

Werner, K. Patricia and J. P. Nelson(2007). *Mosaic 2: grammar*(silver ed.). NY: McGrow-Hill.

Woods, Edward(2002). *The communicative grammar of English workbook*. NY: Pearson Education.

박미숙

이화여자대학교 대학원 영어영문학과 박사과정 졸업
(음성음운론 전공, 문학박사)
현재 목원대학교 사범대학 영어교육과 교수

대학생을 위한 기본영문법

초판 1쇄 발행 _ 2019년 11월 20일
초판 2쇄 발행 _ 2024년 9월 2일

저　　자 • 박 미 숙
발 행 인 • 정 현 걸
발　　행 • 신 아 사
인　　쇄 • 대명프린팅
출판등록 • 1956년 1월 5일 (제9-52호)
주　　소 • 서울특별시 은평구 통일로 59길 4 (2층)
전　　화 • 02)382-6411 · 팩스 02)382-6401
홈페이지 • www.shinasa.co.kr
E-MAIL • shinasa@daum.net

ISBN 978-89-8396-352-9 (93740)

정가 14,000원